The Trouble with Play

The Trouble with Play

Susan Grieshaber and Felicity McArdle

Open University Press

Open University Press
McGraw-Hill Education
McGraw-Hill House
Shoppenhangers Road
Maidenhead
Berkshire
England
SL6 2QL

email: enquiries@openup.co.uk
world wide web: www.openup.co.uk

and Two Penn Plaza, New York, NY 10121-2289, USA

First published 2010

A catalogue record of this book is available from the British Library

ISBN-13: 978-0-33-523791-3 (pb) 978-0-33-523790-6 (hb)
ISBN-10: 0335237916 (pb) 0335237908 (hb)

Library of Congress Cataloging-in-Publication Data
CIP data applied for

Typeset by RefineCatch Limited, Bungay, Suffolk
Printed in the UK by Bell & Bain Ltd, Glasgow

Fictitious names of companies, products, people, characters and/or data that may
be used herein (in case studies or in examples) are not intended to represent any
real individual, company, product or event.

The **McGraw·Hill** Companies

Contents

Acknowledgements

We acknowledge the support of Professor Carmel Diezmann, Assistant Dean Research, Centre for Learning Innovation in the Faculty of Education at Queensland University of Technology. A small research grant from the Centre for Learning Innovation enabled the collection of data for this project. We recognize the skill of the research assistant, Melinda Miller, in capturing the play episodes and engaging with practitioners about what was occurring. Both of us are also appreciative of the support from Professor Ann Farrell, Head, School of Early Childhood, Queensland University of Technology, who provided practical assistance that helped us get the job done. The conversations with Eva Johansson and Airi Bigsten about the Swedish preschool curriculum were very informative, and thanks to Jo Carr for spontaneously suggesting the title for this work during a serendipitous chat!

Dedications

This book is dedicated to the goal of fair play.
For Zac and Kate and the fun of playing around.
And for Valerie McArdle who, at the age of eighty-seven years, is a player and a stayer.

1 The meaning of play in early childhood education

Play as learning?

> Virtually all early childhood educators (and many others) espouse play as a sacred right of childhood, as the way in which young human beings learn, as a major avenue through which children learn to be happy, mentally healthy human beings.
>
> G. S. Cannella, *Deconstructing Early Childhood Education: Social Justice and Revolution*

The Trouble with Play departs from some of the ideas about play that are held dear by many in early childhood education. It raises questions around fairness and calls for teachers to understand and implement more equitable approaches to play in the early years. We acknowledge that while play does have many benefits for children, it is often promoted as a universal and almost magical 'fix' in the early years. In other words, the adage that children are 'learning through play' might have a great deal of truth attached to it, but it is time to look more deeply at what is being learned, and how that learning is occurring. For many practitioners who work with young children and their families, play is the supreme and necessary ingredient in children's development and learning. We agree that play provides a wide range of potential opportunities for children to learn and develop. However, there are some ideas associated with play in early childhood education that seem to be accepted almost without question. These include the ideas that play is natural, normal, innocent, fun, solely about development and learning, beneficial to all children, and a universal right for children.

We challenge these taken-for-granted understandings of play in early childhood education and argue that play in the early years is not always innocent and fun; that it is also political and involves morals and ethics. Further, there are other sides to play that are not so romantic, natural, or particularly educative, and play is not always the best way for young children to learn. From these perspectives, we systematically take apart some long-held beliefs about play, and expose understandings and meanings of play that have been silenced or made invisible.

In this chapter we develop the argument that if play-based approaches in early childhood education are to contribute to an equitable future, then we need to:

- challenge some dearly held and often unquestioned beliefs about play;
- create ways of working with play that are more equitable, fair and just for all children;
- avoid the type of play that privileges those children who are already positioned more powerfully by factors such as social and cultural capital, gender, size, ethnicity and proficiency with English.

To do this we call on history as well as current perspectives and recontextualize play, taking it out of the psychological and development framework, and repositioning it as a cultural and historical construction, for better or worse. We draw on relevant literature to consider the various meanings that have been associated with play in the early years, locate them in historical and cultural perspectives, and provide an analysis of how play has come to assume the significance it has. As such our aim is not to review the huge corpus of literature about play.

The goals for this chapter are to:

- identify and analyse highly valued beliefs about play, such as play being natural, that it is about development and learning, that it is fun, innocent and a universal right;
- reposition play as a cultural and historical construction and analyse how it has come to be the mainstay of early childhood education.

We begin by considering highly valued beliefs about play and analysing them in terms of social and cultural constructions. Understandings about play are linked inextricably to constructions of children and childhood, both historical and contemporary. While we focus on play, where relevant we discuss constructions of children and childhood. Highly valued beliefs include the ideas that play is:

- natural;
- about development and learning;
- normal;
- fun;
- innocent;
- a universal right for children.

These highly valued beliefs are all closely connected. We discuss each and show how these ideas have come to assume the importance they have in the early years of the twenty-first century.

Play is natural

The ideas of Jean-Jacques Rousseau (born in Switzerland in 1712) have been particularly influential in understanding play in early childhood education. Rousseau was inspired by Plato's ideas about growth and development being 'the unfolding of innate ideas' (Weber 1984: 31). As a romantic naturalist, Rousseau (1762/2007) initiated a romantic stream of thinking based on the biological metaphors of health and growth. He challenged ideas of the time by rejecting the Christian notion of original sin and promoting a belief in innate human goodness. Accordingly, Rousseau advocated freedom, naturalism, growth, interest, activity, and originality. He believed that children were most likely to experience healthy development if they were guided by nature, rather than by the influence of society. Ideas such as children being naturally good, that they should have freedom to play, and that play is a natural thing for children, originated with Rousseau. He saw the purpose of education as enabling the inherent goodness of children to unfold, as he believed in developing the potential of each unique individual, which would then lead to a society that was more harmonious and less restrictive, with more freedom. Rousseau supported the notion of noninterference with children and their development because of an innate driving force that enables them to make wise decisions without adult interference (Cleverley and Phillips 1987). Rousseau's advice to mothers embodied freedom and naturalism as he encouraged them to 'let them [children] eat, run and play as much as they want' (Rousseau 1762/ 2007: 103). Likewise, he encouraged mothers to 'trust the child's spontaneous impulses' (Weber 1984: 27).

Émile (Rousseau 1762/2007) is Rousseau's most well known book about child development and education. It was banned and burned publicly on publication but it became a European best seller and has survived to be an enduring influence on early childhood education. *Émile* depicts a fictional boy whom Rousseau proposed to tutor using nature's plan for healthy development: 'Nature is like a hidden tutor who prompts the child to develop different capacities at different stages of growth' (Crain 2005: 13). Rousseau was the first to introduce the idea of stages of child development. To ensure that individuals developed to their full potential, nature and the four stages of development need to work together. Because of the emphasis on the influence of nature, Rousseau privileged nature over nurture. In *Émile*, Rousseau (1762/2007: 108) raised the work/play dichotomy, commenting: 'Work and play are all the one for him [*Émile*], his games are his work; he knows no difference. He brings to everything the cheerfulness of interest, the charm of freedom, and he shows the bent of his own mind and the extent of his knowledge.'

As can be seen from this comment, to Rousseau, play and work are the same thing. The significance Rousseau attached to interest and freedom are also apparent. Émile can see no difference between work and play because he is interested in games and adults will not be intervening in them. As Rousseau reasoned, this creates a certain freedom that enables Émile to express his ideas and show his knowledge through play. As with many books written around this time, *Émile* was about education for the sons of the rich: Rousseau was not concerned about education for girls or the poor. Rousseau's ideas were new at the time and they invoked a different philosophy of education – what is called 'child-centred education' today (Crain 2005).

While Rousseau wrote much about education, he did not put his ideas into practice. Despite this, many of Rousseau's ideas still influence early childhood education today. These include the connection between play, freedom and nature, or play as a natural thing for children to do; the lack of interference from adults in children's development, and work and play being the same. However, the most significant point for *The Trouble with Play* is that *Émile*, Rousseau's most famous and influential treatise about child development and education, was a lengthy book of fiction. Further, he had five children and placed them all in a state foundling home. He was soundly criticized for these actions and as a result, many have refused to take his ideas about education seriously (Crain 2005). However, the fiction of *Émile* and his own actions as a parent have not interfered with the way in which his ideas have been embraced in early childhood education. The point is that the field has placed a large and enduring stake on something based entirely on fiction.

Play, development and learning

The centrality of play in children's learning comes from Comenius (1592–1670), who understood the importance of young children learning in an environment that 'encourages playful activity' (Fein 1999: 194). Following Comenius, Pestalozzi (1746–1827) retained an emphasis on play but added objects that could be manipulated and used a sensory approach to curriculum. Along with other educators, sociologists, biologists and psychologists, Froebel is among those who viewed play in terms of its contribution to children's growth and development. Froebel was probably the first to create what we might now call a curriculum for the early years, which was influenced by those who came before him. Our interest is in how he saw play, which was, according to Weber (1984: 37), 'the perfect medium for self-activity – for the release of the child's inner powers.' Belief in releasing the child's inner powers is suggestive of Rousseau's (1762/2007) thoughts about enabling the inherent goodness of children to unfold. In Froebel's (1900: 11) terms, self-activity involved the 'whole self . . . in all phases of being'. The concept of holistic development and concern with the whole child is part and parcel of contemporary approaches to early childhood education.

Like Rousseau (1762/2007), Froebel (1900: 58) saw connections between work and play, with Froebel acknowledged as having '. . . found the true nature and function of play, and of regulating it in such a way as to lead it naturally and gradually into work, securing for work the same spontaneity and joy, the same freedom and serenity, that characterize the plays of childhood.'

The esteem that Froebel (1900: 54–5) held for the value of play cannot be underestimated. He linked its value directly with child and human development:

> Play is the highest phase of child development – of human development at this period . . . It gives therefore, joy, freedom, contentment, inner and outer rest, peace with the world. It holds the sources of all that is good . . . Is not the most beautiful expression of child-life at this time a playing child? – a child wholly absorbed in his [sic] play? – a child that has fallen asleep while so absorbed?
>
> . . . play at this time is not trivial, it is highly serious and of deep significance. Cultivate and foster it, O mother; protect and guard it, O father! . . .
>
> The plays of childhood are the germinal leaves of all later life; for the whole man [sic] is developed and shown in these . . .

Froebel's words illustrate his exuberance for play and the significance he attached to it. This and the previous excerpt also shows how play connects closely to other revered ideas in early childhood education associated with play: joy, freedom, spontaneity. It provides evidence of aspects of play that remain highly valued in early childhood education today. However, Froebel ignored what Sutton-Smith (1997: 132) called 'dark play', possibly because of the influence of the Romantic movement and its emphasis on freedom, nature and the innocence of children. But in doing this a precedent was set for what followed, which ensured that the emphasis on freedom, nature and the innocence of children's play was maintained.

Attributing children's development, joy, freedom, contentment and peace to play is suggestive of play as a universal remedy, as the solution for successful child (and human) development. Froebel (1900) did say that play 'holds the sources' of all that is good and that the plays of childhood set the stage for later life. Historicism, the idea of progress as inevitable and achievable in society, came together in the eighteenth century with evolution and created the idea that child development 'could also be seen as a form of progress and adaptation' (Sutton-Smith 1997: 19). Child development became a way in which children's progress and adaptation was made visible, and play is an intrinsic part of this observable growth and development. The combination of historicism and romantic notions of play have been instrumental in cementing the relationship between play and development, making it almost impossible to talk about play without development in early childhood education. In fact Sutton-Smith (1997: 36) goes as far as saying that 'the relationship between play and development has become so taken for granted that it is invoked almost any time an investigator finds an analogy between a play process and some other developmental process.' The overwhelming reverence for the value and benefits of play, evident in the early work of Comenius and Froebel, has steered the place of play in early childhood education for more than 150 years. The relationship between play and development has been so influential that now 'People simply take it for granted . . . that children develop as a result of their playing' (Sutton-Smith 1997: 11–12).

Play is normal

Over many years, the notion of play as a normal part of childhood and a normal part of what occurs in early childhood settings has occurred through the creation of a specific language of play and knowledge about play (Ailwood 2003). Ailwood claims that this language 'enables talk and thought about what is *normal* play, including understandings of age-based phases of play and types of play' (Ailwood 2003: 295; emphasis in original). The idea that play is central to young children's learning (Comenius), that play is a natural activity (Rousseau 1762/2007), and Froebel's (1900) endorsement of the value and benefit of play for children's development and learning were foundational in establishing play as a 'normal' activity for children. So, too, was the association between play and child development, established as representing progress: children 'adapt and develop through their play' (Sutton-Smith 1997: 9). However, as Sutton-Smith (1997: 9) notes, the relevance of play to progress has been more often assumed than demonstrated.

As an example of what is assumed rather than demonstrated in regard to play and progress, the following excerpt illustrates not only how dramatic play is considered a normal part of play for preschool children but also the way in which the development of skills is assumed to occur. It describes the activities of children in a preschool class in the USA as they engaged in a dramatic play area established as part of reading stories from the picture books of Laura Ingalls Wilder's *Little House on the Prairie*: 'As children play, they gain communication and negotiation skills; if conflicts arise, they engage in creative problem solving. Dramatic play fosters resilience as children realize they must be flexible in order for the play to continue' (Miles 2009: 37–8).

In this excerpt, the understanding is that play is a part of normal everyday activities for the preschool children ('As children play . . .'). There is also an unquestioned assumption that the very act of playing produces an automatic increase in children's communication and negotiation skills. This is an example of the power of the language of play and knowledge about play: there is no need to justify or provide an explanation of how these skills might increase because of the common sense understandings about play that exist (see Sutton-Smith 1997). However, there is no consideration of the type or appropriateness of the skills that are gained as a result of engaging in play. Instead a blanket assumption gives the impression that whatever the skills, they will be advantageous.

Likewise, there is a supposition that, if conflicts arise, children engage instinctively in creative problem solving: they will naturally know what to do to resolve the conflict. This harks back to Rousseau's (1972/2007) ideas of not intervening in play because children's innate driving force will enable them to make wise decisions if not interfered with by adults. There is no suggestion of conflict being resolved by surreptitious means that might relate to gender, socio-economic status, size, age, or any number of other factors that impact children's interactions in play; and which have been documented qualitatively (see, for example, Walkerdine 1981; Thorne 1993; Skattebol 2005; Mundine and Giugni 2006). The excerpt also suggests that resilience is something all children must have, no matter what. What might be compromised in the name of flexibility is not given a second thought. The prime consideration is that the play continues – who benefits and who has to make concessions, and the nature of those concessions is not mentioned. These are the very things that reveal the power relations that are at work in children's play; they are the factors that can result in some children being marginalized and others privil-eged. When play is seen as a normal part of early childhood programmes, it is attributed with special features such as enabling innate and creative problem solving, as illustrated in this example (Miles 2009). However, not all play is beneficial for all children at all times and approaches that suggest this are naïve because they neglect the power relations that operate in all interactions, including those that are at work in children's everyday play.

Play is fun

Ideas about play being fun go back for centuries and are illustrative of Ailwood's (2003) contention about the development of a specific language of play and knowledge about play. Comenius talked about playful activity (Fein 1999) and associated 'delight' with play (Weber 1984); Rousseau (1762/2007: 108) referred to 'cheerfulness' and he also mentioned 'freedom' in relation to children's play. Like Rousseau, Froebel (1900) used the word 'freedom' but he also talked about spontaneity and joy when describing children's play.

'Fun' seems to be the twentieth- and twenty-first-century version of joy and cheerfulness. As part of the education revolution promised by the Prime Minister of Australia (Rudd 2008), the Commonwealth government 'will ensure all four year olds have access to 15 hours of fun, play-based early education a week, for 40 weeks a year.' Qualified early childhood teachers will provide the fun, play-based education. The Prime Minister is not alone in thinking that early childhood education should be fun and play-based. This connection pervades contemporary writing about early childhood education:

- 'Play/project based classrooms provide a learning environment that is a rich invitation to children to explore, investigate, experiment and discover that learning is fun, productive and achievable for all.' (Walker 2006: 51)
- 'Fun! Fun! Fun! They have to have fun! If they're not having fun, then send them home! It's not worth it, you know. It's a waste. When you're four years old and you're not having fun? Come on.' (Lee 2006: 435)
- 'Parents' definitions of play in this study are that play is fun.' (Vickerius and Sandberg 2006: 212)

The link between play and fun is an integral part of the knowledge about play that has been encapsulated in the specific language of play. At the same time, this link enables talk about play being fun and central to development and learning, and perpetuates a powerful discourse that play should be fun for children.

The discourse of play as fun succeeds in making invisible or silencing play that is not fun. The rhetorics of child play dictate that children develop, through play, skills that enable them to continue to play successfully, which in turn generates happiness (Sutton-Smith 1997). Successful playing then gives rise to further successful play experiences. But what of 'dark play' (Sutton-Smith 1997) and those children who do not have successful play experiences (and are therefore not happy)? Not all play is fun, as Walkerdine (1981) and others have shown. Play is also the very serious business of childhood where power relations are played out in terms of 'race', class, socio-economic status, gender, ethnicity, age, size, skin colour, sexuality, heteronormativity, proficiency with English, and more (Grieshaber 2008a). If play reproduces what children experience in their daily lives, then it can mean rejection, discomfort and alienation for some children. In fact some children are 'so motivated to be accepted in play that they make sacrifices . . . for membership in the group' (Sutton-Smith 1997: 43). What, then, is conceded in the politics of play? What is traded, what is won and lost, by who, how, and why? Because power relations are involved in children's interactions with each other and with adults, play does not always provide the type of fun ascribed to it in much early childhood literature and discourse.

Play is innocent

The concepts of innocence and play have coalesced, predicated by Rousseau's beliefs in romantic naturalism. When Rousseau (1762/2007) rejected the Christian notion of original sin in preference for guidance from nature, he confirmed the innocence of the child. Children's inner selves were to unfold in conjunction with play and the virtues of nature, and they were to be protected from the damaging effects of society. This amounted to the creation of childhood as a period of innocence and dependency (Burman 2008) and it explains the overwhelming preference for concentrating on the positive sides of play. However these ideas were put aside with industrialization in Britain in the late eighteenth century and the use of child labour in factories. Nevertheless, as Hendrick (1997: 40) points out, critics of *laissez-faire* capitalism voiced the value of a ' "natural" and "innocent" childhood'. When the need for child labour ended and mass schooling was introduced, another version of childhood innocence emerged – one that drew on the eighteenth-century understanding of child nature (Hendrick 1997). Children were thus constituted as dependent through mass schooling and, according to Burman (2008: 74), subjected to 'a middle-class ideal of childhood as a period of helplessness'. Working-class children were positioned as ignorant and in need of education and socialization (Burman 2008), and the innocent child of the eighteenth and nineteenth centuries became the inspiration for contemporary approaches to child-centred education (James, Jenks and Prout 1998).

Child-centred education valorizes play and childhood innocence, preserving earlier ideas of freedom and the unfolding of children's inner selves but adding an emphasis on children's needs and interests. It grew from social, educational and economic factors, such as the harsh 'payment by results' approach of primary schools in the latter stages of the nineteenth century; the rejection of rote teaching methods and behaviourist (empty vessel) approaches (Burman 2008); the emphasis on 'love' and 'nature', and the 'production of development as pedagogy' (Walkerdine 1984: 162). In child-centred education children are given choices about the type of play in which they engage but it is to be an 'enjoyable, self-directed, non-goal oriented' activity (Burman 2008: 263). There is little intervention in children's play or development because practitioners are facilitators; thus concepts and skills 'discovered' through play may be inaccurate. Like other dubious aspects of child-centred education, there is no solution to this quandary apart from the possibility of the child coming to accurate understandings through further play and 'discoveries'. Thus the combination of play and innocence has significant pedagogical implications. However, the pervasiveness of the play-innocence duo has resulted in many authors using children's play as a metaphor 'for what is innocent' (Sutton-Smith 1997: 2). Further, because it is established on notions of innocence, play that is coercive, cruel and dangerous is ignored (Burman 2008).

A recent concern about the loss of children's innocence was evident in England with the introduction of the National Curriculum (from 1988 on). According to Wood (2007b: 123), there was an outcry from the early childhood community about subject matter: 'we teach children not subjects', as if subject matter content was a contaminant of young people's innocence, rather than being the essential building blocks of their learning, progress and achievements'.

Play is a universal right

As an integral part of child-centred education, play emerged as one of several rights proclaimed by child advocates during the twentieth century: 'a universal childhood with rights and special needs ... The right to health and education, the right to play and to freedom from work' (Silin 1995: 121). The right of all children to engage in play is enshrined in Article 31 of the United Nations Convention on the Rights of the Child (UNCRC). The Convention was adopted in 1989 and has been ratified by all countries with the exception of the United States and Somalia. Here we want to point out the distinctly Western perspective that is enveloped in the Convention and some of the difficulties associated with it that relate to play. Burr (2002: 49) puts it succinctly when she says that the UNCRC 'assumes that children are universally the same. It can be argued that its provisions are weighted in favour of a modern, western sense of the individual.' The first point, the assumption of a one-size-fits-all approach, takes no account of children's vastly different social, economic, cultural and political circumstances around the globe. Treating children as an homogeneous group shows little understanding of differences that exist in the life circumstances of children.

The second point made by Burr (2002) about the UNCRC adopting a modern Western sense of the individual is problematic for anyone whose perspectives of children and children's rights are not based on these same principles. The trouble is that it is another form of domination by the West (north?) and invokes notions of colonialism because of the lack of respect for philosophical positions not prefaced by Western versions of individualism. This includes belief systems where families are considered to be more important than individuals and the ideal that all children should be living in a family context, preferably their own. In terms of the universal right of all children to play, the applicability of the Convention is questionable for children who have no choice between working and starving, which is an economic rather than ideological matter. Street children are particularly disturbing because they challenge Western notions of what constitutes an appropriate childhood and the belief that children are in need of adult protection (Stephens 1995; Burr 2002). Further, the way that play is privileged in many Western early childhood settings and its close links with growth and development can be inconsistent with some non-Western views about children and learning. Accepting that play is a universal right is therefore a culturally specific belief that favours Western ways of viewing children and childhood.

One of the outcomes of the movement of people around the globe is that many early childhood settings reflect a much more diverse clientele than they did even in the late 1990s. Because globalization is a fact of life, having produced 'mobile and heterogeneous, multilingual and multicultural populations . . . conventional models of child development and their normative models of childcare, schooling and early education' have been called into question (Luke and Grieshaber 2004: 8). In these circumstances, what happens in early childhood settings should be shaped by the context as well as the specific students with whom practitioners are working on a daily basis (Grieshaber 2008b). Thus early childhood teachers need strategies for dealing with diverse populations who bring varying experiences that may range from war trauma, poverty and starvation to religious persecution, and include families with varying degrees of education and English-language proficiency. Even in relatively homogeneous populations, there are gender, socio-economic, religious and cultural differences, and those who work with young children are obligated to provide environments where equitable approaches are enacted.

Audience

This book is aimed at undergraduate students completing teacher and other qualifications such as diploma courses, which will enable them to work in early childhood settings. It also has direct relevance for those working in the field as well as postgraduate students who are interested in reading about alternative perspectives on play. For practitioners who are committed to social justice, *The Trouble with Play* helps identify and recognize injustice that occurs in play. It shows how injustice is sustained by taken-for-granted structures, practices, relationships, and discourses that are an integral part of everyday life, and how these structures and so on work to privilege some groups and marginalize others (Ryan and Grieshaber 2005). Hyland (in press) has pointed out that in the USA, those enrolled in teacher education courses are mainly 'White, middle class women who go into teaching because they love children or want a job that fits well with family life, rather than out of a desire to challenge the existing social order'. Hyland claims that many teacher education students in the USA are reluctant to accept 'the basic premise of social justice education – that society is fundamentally unjust'. We suggest that this is quite possibly the case in other countries as well. *The Trouble with Play* challenges some highly valued and taken-for-granted beliefs and practices about play. Through scenarios and vignettes, it identifies alternative ways of seeing, thinking, understanding and doing. These are not always moments of tension or conflict, such as children hitting each other. They can be moments that practitioners might not think are significant at all because they are everyday and 'common sense' understandings and unquestioned ways of doing things. However, these moments provide opportunities for contesting, challenging and renegotiating the way things are and the way things might be. They may lead to difficult conversations, conflict and tension about play and its relation to social justice. We hope that we can prompt practitioners to think again about some 'tried and true', highly valued and accepted ways of talking about and 'doing' play in early childhood education.

The scenarios and vignettes

The examples used in this book are drawn from a range of sources. They include previously published works, experiences from our own engagement with young children in early childhood settings, and scenarios gathered through a small research project undertaken as part of writing this book. The research project received approval from the Queensland University of Technology Human Research Ethics Committee (approval number 0900000909). Data were gathered by video recording children at three long-day child care centres in the city of Brisbane, Australia during 2009. Two centres are for-profit enterprises and one centre operated on a not-for-profit basis. Approximately 50 children from the three centres were video and audio recorded engaging in daily activities. Where possible, in addition to written consent from parents, verbal permission from individual children was sought before recording began. However, it was not possible to gain verbal consent from very young children, especially those aged two or younger, when recording their actions and activities. Eighteen practitioners were involved in informal conversations about play. Debriefing also occurred at the end of each data recording session. Practitioners and the research assistant viewed the video record of the day and practitioner responses were sought to the play that was occurring.

Outline of the rest of the book

Much of the rhetoric associated with play connects it with fun, and as good and wholesome for all concerned. If play is fun, who is it fun for? In the first part of Chapter 2, 'Play as fun; play as hard work', we examine ideas of play as fun and investigate links with adult-centred ideas that are wrapped up in the romance of idealized childhoods of times past, often based on notions of innocence. Childhoods today are not the same as those past and, indeed, the nostalgic views of childhoods past are largely myths. The second part of this chapter acknowledges that, while play can be fun, it also involves the hard work of negotiating and creating individual subjectivities of who children are, what they can do in this setting, with whom, when and where; and how this is worked out in the complexity of social relations that exist in most early childhood contexts.

In Chapter 3, 'Naturally produced play', we question the idea that play is 'natural'. A case is made that play is a cultural construction and is read as an indicator of a happy healthy childhood. But for play to look and appear natural it can require that children have to learn and be taught how to play in certain ways. This means that the 'natural' is manufactured in particular ways to achieve certain ends. The case for play as a cultural construction is supported by considering examples that are opposite to the notion of play as natural. The key idea explored in Chapter 4, 'The glamour of play: play as serious business', is the glamour and romance of young children's play, and the collapsing of young children's art with play. The idea that children's play is natural makes a neat fit with how modernist artists saw young children's art as being natural, spontaneous, free, about self-expression, and untaught. Just as Chapter 1 introduced questions around the *laissez-faire* approach to children's play, the second part of Chapter 4 explores the powerful taboos around 'teaching' art with young children.

As Chapter 5 ('Play rules: rules for play') indicates, play 'rules' in many early childhood settings, while in many others, it doesn't. No matter the type of play that occurs, the rules for play are often (but not always) established by adults such as teachers and assistants. In this chapter we consider some adult rules about play, which include bans on things such as guns, play that is too messy or dirty, and play that is risky. Much play in early childhood settings reproduces the status quo. That is, it reproduces what exists in society in terms of relations of power about gender, skin colour, social, economic and cultural capital, ethnicity, heteronormativity, and proficiency with English. Chapter 6, 'Fair play: playing fair', uses examples from practice to make a case for staff and children to learn what fair play is, how to play fair, and how to teach about what fairness in play means. We also argue for early childhood settings to embody policies and actions that include attention to fairness in play at all times, and to enact these policies in daily work.

The place of play in curriculum documents is considered in Chapter 7, 'Play and early childhood curriculum documents.' Documents for children in the years before compulsory schooling are considered from four countries: Hong Kong, Australia, Sweden and England. The place accorded to play, the connections between play and learning, and the ways in which play is to be enacted in the curriculum are investigated. The chapter investigates constructions of play that are articulated in this book (play as natural, play as fun, play as serious business, play as learning, and so on) and their implications for fair play in settings that use these documents. Chapter 8, 'End play', poses a series of eight challenges to play that have been raised throughout the book. What if play is not natural, is not fun, and kids really do make the rules? We hope that these questions and the rest of this book are thought provoking enough for readers to consider other ways of thinking about and 'doing' play in early childhood settings.

2   Play as fun: play as hard work

Ivan arrived in the morning with a large book on Star Wars. The book was filled with glossy photographs of various space machines and he was particularly taken with 'pods' – space capsules for travel through space. He quickly teamed up with his two friends, Thomas and Robert, and they huddled over the book together. At the teacher's prompting, they began constructing a pod, using a large cardboard box. They were busily occupied for the next 60 minutes, cutting windows in the box, lining the interior with various dials and switches, using junk materials like lids, egg cartons, and so on.

At 'critique time', children all came together and shared with each other what they had been doing. When it came to Ivan's turn, he talked about the pod, and when the teacher asked if he was pleased with his efforts, he replied: 'No. Robert says it doesn't look like a pod.' The teacher was surprised, and Robert looked askance, as all eyes turned to him.

The teacher tut-tutted, and said: 'Oh. How did that make you feel Ivan?'

Ivan replied: 'It made me want to make it better.'

Ivan's last comment disrupted a number of taken-for-granted assumptions about what was happening in the classroom. Later in this chapter, we return to Ivan's story, and analyse it through a number of lenses, in order to examine the various discourses at work here. As discussed in Chapter 1, a number of contingencies and ambiguities arise when attempts are made to understand and defend play in early childhood contexts. Ivan's teacher was a staunch advocate for a play-based curriculum, which centred on the children and their interests. Much of her work – the organization of the environment, her planning and preparation, and her interactions with the children, and her observations – were all soundly informed by her understandings of the benefits of play for children's learning, and her role in supporting this play-based approach to teaching and learning. In this chapter, our question is not simply 'is it play' or even 'what is play?' but rather 'what does this belief in the benefits of play do?' If the teacher insists that children learn through play, and play is equated with fun, what does this do? What is allowed and not allowed when 'logic' dictates that learning is fun. How do these beliefs shape the teacher's practices, and the children's actions?

We look particularly at the binary logic that separates *play* from *work*, *fun* from *effort*, and *pleasure* from *pain*. This discursive organization sets up practices that can both enable and constrain what teachers do on a daily basis. Ivan's words actually bring together some of the ambiguities that can cause confusion when early childhood educators resolutely defend the claim that children 'learn through play' and 'learning is fun'.

Chapter goals

- First, we examine the fun/work divide and how this particular binary logic enables and constrains ways of speaking children, learning and teaching.
- Next, we consider what happens when teachers line up with either side of this divide, or work at 'solutions' that attempt to address the ambiguities.
- Finally, we propose ways of thinking that make it possible to plan for young children's learning that makes room for play as fun and hard work, and how this can act for better and worse.

Play as fun

In this section of this chapter, we step out of early childhood education, and take a look at some big-picture discourses of play. Attempts to examine and define play are like defining other big ideas in society – religion, art, peace. Modernist thinking uses binary logic to impose order in our constructions of meaning. In attempts to define play, it is sometimes easier to say what play is not. The factory is the place for work; the playground is not. Weekdays are for work; weekends are not. Work is serious; play is not. In the following chapters, we explore some of these divides in more detail. In this chapter, we look especially at the distinctions that equate play with fun, and therefore insist that work is its opposite. When it is a taken-for-granted assumption that work and fun are opposites, like the factory and the playground, it follows that certain 'rules' emerge about what happens, when and where. However, when play is equated with fun, we can quickly think of examples that 'break the rules'.

In his book *The Ambiguity of Play*, Brian Sutton-Smith (1997) critiques play theories as being more about the theories than the actual act of playing. Just as it is possible to theorize about religion through the eyes of psychology, sociology, and anthropology, so too various theories of play can be constructed. However, the risk is that grand theories can attribute false importance and false explanations. As John Berger (1982) points out in his discussion of art, a bogus religiosity can be attached to artworks, insisting that they are hung in galleries with gilt frames and soft lighting, suggesting that they are more than what they are. Marcel du Champs made this point when he took a second look at art by drawing a moustache on a reproduction of the *Mona Lisa* (see Chapter 4 for more on the modernist artists and their 'play' with the rules of art). In this chapter, we are urging a second look at some of the thinking around play as fun.

Some branches of psychology take an interest in play. The old adage 'all work and no play makes Jack a dull boy' indicates a belief in a healthy life balance, and having fun is necessary for good health. A belief in the importance of recreation, vacations, pleasure time and activities all help the leisure and tourism industries thrive. People who suffer from depression are probably considered to be missing fun, and therapy can be designed and administered to bring fun back into their lives. Here fun is a matter of feelings, and is coupled with feelings of pleasure and joy, self esteem, health and development. Laughter and humour indicate fun, and measures of stress levels have been shown to be lowered by laughter. The simple slapstick humour of the clown has been famously introduced in hospitals, and has been proven to influence the health of the patients directly. Having fun can improve your health.

A more nuanced understanding of fun as feelings of joy and pleasure can also be individual, quiet and profound experiences – for instance, people can enjoy music, painting, theatre, cooking, swimming, or other leisure pastimes. It is here that the use of language becomes more complex, perhaps confusing. Why, for instance, do we speak of playing football, playing the violin, playing cards, but not playing cooking, nor playing swimming? And while there is obviously joy to be had in playing or watching a game of football for some, there is seldom an expectation of laughter or humour.

Challenge and contest can provide joy, pleasure and fun. Here, it is the striving and the challenge to conquer (either oneself or others) that can bring pleasure in the rewards. There are those who find pleasure in hours of training for a race or climbing a mountain. There are, at the same time, others who consider the notion of a 'fun run' an oxymoron (McWilliam and Jones 2005). So fun is contingent on who and what.

Developmental psychology places fun and play as a beginning phase, a developmental stage on the way to eventual mastery. At this point, it is possible simply to have fun, exploring and experimenting, before the hard work, drill, practice and the rules apply. And this learning through play is not confined to children. A colleague recently purchased a new Mac computer and asked about a manual of instructions. She was swiftly told to just take it home and play with it, as that was the best way for her to learn all about her new machine. Corporate organizations sprinkle play throughout their training, and use the fun factor to ensure engagement and interest. Creativity is encouraged through encouragement to 'play with ideas', 'kick some ideas around', 'have some fun to start with, and see what happens'. Google staff members are allocated one day a week to 'play' with ideas and projects away from their everyday work (see Chapter 4 for more on play and creativity).

But while play with a purpose can bring pleasure, there is also a way of thinking about play as silliness, frivolous, even chaos and risk. Some see bungee-jumping as foolish and risky but there are those who seek their fun through the risk and the fear. Designers of joy rides in amusement parks work to find the point between fear and fun. There are those who seek the thrill of not knowing. Gambling is fun for those who feel pleasure in being in the hands of fate. And this line of thought can take us to the dark side of play, 'foul play', and the fine line between pleasure and pain. The disturbing images that came out of the notorious Abu Ghraib prison showed American soldiers playing and having fun – something that shocked the sensibilities of all who saw them. Psychologists deal with those who gain joy and pleasure from causing discomfort and, in the extreme, pain. To a far less degree, humour and laughter can be derived from teasing and gossip – fun, but not for all players.

Anthropologists study play as an indicator of cultural beliefs and practices, and take an interest in how people amuse themselves, who plays, and what they play, what they consider fun. Examining toys, games and leisure activities can shape theories about the values and customs of those who engage with them. For instance, historically, children of agrarian communities played with scaled-down implements, presumably building their future capabilities to do the same work as the adults. Fun, play and toys were once considered the domain of children, and worked as separating devices, to better differentiate between the activities of adults and children, and occupations and pastimes. Children were sent off to play, while adults conducted the serious business of making a living. In more contemporary societies, this is not so simple, if it ever was. Phenomena like the Rubik's Cube spread throughout the global community, and are taken up across any number of countries and cultures, ages and occupations.

Sociologists can take an interest in fun and play – how and where play appears and is 'played out'. For instance, when play and fun become a matter for economists, its legitimacy shifts, and permission to have fun is not confined to childhood. In a recent small study inquiring into the social and cultural capital needs of recently arrived refugee children in a school in Australia (McArdle and Tan 2009), researchers identified clear differences between the out-of-school pastimes of children from Africa and children from Korea. Photographs that the children took on the weekend showing how they spent their leisure time indicated that the children from Korea were involved in activities ranging from family outings to a game of golf, and an orchestral concert. The images captured by the children from Africa showed time spent at a skate park, travelling on a train, and going to a local shopping centre. What constitutes play, fun, and leisure for these children is contingent on their social and cultural capital.

Fun and games are also read as indicators of class, status and nationhood. Nations are defined, for some, by the games they play. Cricket, for instance, is played by countries with British colonial histories. The various codes of football, which to many observers do not look like much 'fun', can indicate nationalistic qualities. In fact, one proposal of Sutton-Smith's (1997) is that the fun in football is the permission it gives to visit violence on opponents, a violence not otherwise sanctioned in society. A perhaps kinder theory is that the fun is in the contest. For some, the introduction of competition produces fun – although it has to be said, this fun might only be for those who win competitions. The physicality and the contest of many games is where the fun lies. The international Olympics spectacular might be considered the pinnacle of this version of fun. Athletes at the peak of physical condition compete for honours – for themselves, and their country.

The teaching and learning in many games is also not confined to children. Games like Monopoly teach capitalist values. Chess is considered a game of intellect and patience. Adults play with words and numbers, with crosswords and Sudoku. Facebook and other social networking sites create spaces for playing with identity, and virtual gaming allows for players to produce avatars and interact with others across the globe. There are also those who have fun through the use of humour and laughter to protest against systems and power. People of all ages can have fun with jokes and riddles, which usually involve playing with words. This fun, too, can be either 'innocent', or cruel. Jokes can be simply funny, but they can also be subversive, highlighting the ridiculous and the ironic in accepted norms. Historically, the jesters and clowns of the *carnivale* (Bakhtin 1981) performed this function, and it was the humour and laughter that permitted their acts of subversion. Like play and fun, humour is a slippery concept. Individuals, groups, societies and even governments can be at variance about what is funny, what is not, and when and what humour 'goes too far'. So fun is also contingent on purpose and outcome.

When fun and games are attached to other concepts, they can add status and acceptability to what might otherwise be of concern. Just as the use of the word 'democratic' adds value as a descriptor for multiple models of government, attaching play or games can add capital (such as war games, sex play, mind games). Adding words like 'games' or 'play' can make otherwise unattractive concepts more 'friendly' – for example, word games, maths games, play learning.

In this first section of the chapter, we have not attempted to address every angle there is on play but, rather, we suggest that through the process of scientification (Foucault 2000), theorists have to turn play into an object, and then put it under a microscope to examine its various components. And the components they identify are contingent on the theory or lens being applied. For instance, play might be conceived as purely a function of the body, or a behaviour, a matter for groups or individuals, or an experience, a form of thinking, or a function of language. Radical doubt about any truth claims can help to test and question any and all of these taken-for-granted assumptions that might be associated with play. Or, another way to think about this is to accept that there are many ways of seeing play, and all have some truths. We also want to caution against over-analysis, which might have attributed false importance and false explanations to any of the points we have raised. Our purpose is simply to 'play' with 'play', and encourage an openness to play with the ideas presented.

Serious fun?

At this point we insist that the notion of fun is contingent. Firstly, it depends on who the 'players' are. Whether they are adults, children (babies and toddlers, school aged, adolescents), male or female, groups, or individuals, can qualify 'fun'. For adults, work is about earning a living, and is serious. Fun is not serious. It is about daydreaming, tourism, vacations, television, perhaps gambling. Although there might be embarrassment around calling them play, adults engage with any number of activities outside work – hobbies, pastimes, recreation and entertainment. The tourism and leisure industries have much invested in the need for healthy adults and children (consumers) to play. But this sort of fun is a luxury not available to all adults and children.

Place and time can also make a difference to fun. Children's playgrounds are usually places where squeals of delight can be heard. Children can have fun in the classroom too, but, according to King (1992), no matter what the activity, if it happens inside a classroom, children no longer refer to it as 'play'. While some play and fun is dependent on the presence of a group, other fun involves solitary pursuits – most people prefer to read alone. But is reading work or play? Here is another interesting question – is it the case that information acquired through reading is work but information acquired through film and television is fun? Fun is contingent on who, when and where.

Purpose is usually associated with work, while play is considered less serious. The degree of risk and chance attached to purpose can change the ways in which fun, play and work are seen. The adventurer experiences pleasure and fun through conquering challenges, taking risks, and eventually achieving goals. 'Extreme sports' introduce fear and risk into the mix of pleasure and fun (and pain). The purpose, the difficulty and the determination give legitimacy to the risk and the fun, and high status can be attached to some versions of fun and play. In his book *The Play Ethic*, Pat Kane (2004) proposes that play is the new work, and offers some provocative ways of thinking about the work/play divide in the post-industrial era. He maintains that the line between work and leisure is shifting, and the time spent outside work is increasingly important to healthy living. Kane champions the gains to be had from developing skills through play.

The element of freedom, the degree of choice, and the level of constraints make for further complexities around idea of play and fun. The idea of fun being the pleasure in training, straining, and eventually achieving a goal sits alongside a notion of play as free, unpredictable, risky, beyond control, and in the hands of destiny. Gamblers take their pleasure/pain in playing games that are governed by chance or fate. While building a sandcastle can bring pleasure through the effort, design, completion and aesthetic, some take just as much pleasure and glee in knocking down sandcastles, creating the chaos and uncontrolled destruction – because they can. The chance and unpredictability in this fun can produce the thrill, the freedom, and even the risky play. Running, chasing, catching, squealing with glee, are all sounds of pleasure and fun in a playground. These sounds are different from the fun of the contest, competing, or mastering skills with ball, bat or body. Free choice, uncontrolled outcomes, and destiny are all ideas that sit within this version of fun and play.

In this first part of this chapter, we have raised a number of questions around taken-for-granted ideas about play as fun, and the opposite of work. There is much written about play and we make no attempt to cover all possibilities in any comprehensive way. Our purpose is chiefly to provoke new questions and thinking about play. As foregrounded in Chapter 1, the use of the word 'play' can mean different things, and this is not easy to pin down. In this chapter, we attach the word 'fun' with the word 'play', and examine what this does, what it allows, and what it does not permit. But this is not a simple matter of devising a new binary for thinking play. For instance, if you are described as a 'player', this can have either positive or negative connotations. 'Gamers' currently enjoy high status in some circles. If someone is judged as insincere or manipulative, they can be described as a 'player'. If someone is considered an important person in their field, and going places, they too can be described as a 'player'. And these ambiguities are part of your own daily activities. You might play an online game. You might learn a new program on your computer by 'playing' with its features. You might play with your identity on *Facebook*, or other online networks. These three examples of play are all very different activities, and involve different processes, feelings, 'rules', pleasures and rewards. And you can probably think of many more ways that you play each day. So play is not confined to children. We discuss this point in more detail in Chapter 3.

Having played in the messiness of defining play, fun and work, we now zoom in on early childhood education as a contingent site, and look for ways in which educators try to make sense of these competing, conflicting and sometimes complementary ideas, as they go about their work of caring for young children, and educating them. This is not done in order to find a neat fit, or an explanation that will establish a level of comfort and clarity. Rather, we want to highlight the complexities, and bring these understandings to our common goals of equity and success for all the children with whom we work. This is not a search for the best theory or the best explanation. In this next section, we ask what work these theories do. How do they shape the everyday practices and activities in early childhood settings? Who are the players and who are the played? And how can we use these understandings to help provide quality experiences for the young children in our care?

We should also pause and remind you of the call for radical doubt about any truth claims, including any we might make in this chapter. Also recall Sutton-Smith's (1997) wariness about false importance and false explanations, through the use of the theories we apply in our analysis of Ivan's story. This is not an excuse, nor a collapsing into relativity. Rather, it is a call for the recognition of complexities, multiplicities, and the need for flexibility, depth of understanding, and a willingness to research and to reflect on our practices, not to rely on slogans and mantras to account for the work we do.

Making learning fun?

When early childhood educators are urged to make learning fun for young children, a cacophony of voices can shape what this means. In some countries (such as the USA, the UK, and Australia) it appears that we are losing the battle for play in early childhood settings. Regimes of standardized testing, deliverable outcomes and the prioritizing of the more traditional literacy, numeracy and science teaching have seen the academic push-down which leaves little time or space for the long-established practices of play-based learning. Ironically, this is occurring at a time when other countries (China, Singapore and Vietnam) urge their early childhood educators to introduce more playful approaches to teaching and learning. Centres in Sweden and Italy sustain their advocacy for play in the early years. Early childhood educators use a number of strategies in defence of play but, as we will see in Ivan's story, many arguments only serve to reinforce the binary thinking, and do nothing to disrupt the powerful lines along which the battle is being fought. In this next section, we revisit Ivan's story, which began this chapter, and consider the conglomeration of theories and discourses that might be intersecting and colliding, as teachers and the children go about their day.

On the one hand, developmental psychologists would see much to celebrate in Ivan's story. Early childhood educators, child development specialists, and some parents, firmly believe that play is the best way for children to learn. They would see that Ivan is having fun, playing with his friends. They are happy, not squabbling or arguing, engaged with a task that stems from their own interest in *Star Wars*, connected with their lifeworlds and popular culture. It could be argued that, through play, Ivan, Thomas and Robert are developing important concepts, skills, and attitudes, which lay the foundations for life-long learning. When they are engaged in this play, they are thinking, solving problems, experimenting, taking risks, communicating, and trying out new ideas. This is the version of fun that comes with the pleasure and joy of striving, grappling with challenges, even getting 'hot and sweaty' with their efforts, and intrinsic motivation. The reward is in their achievement and effort. They draw on a whole repertoire of simulations, repetitions, games, laughter, and enjoyment, as they learn. Learning in this way will lead to later successes in school, and beyond.

On the other hand, some school administrators, teachers, parents and politicians would see this play as a waste of time, off-task behaviour ('they're just playing around'), needless coddling of children, messy, noisy, unstructured and uneducational, an unaffordable luxury in an ever more competitive world. They would consider this activity as antithetical to effective learning. The puritan idea of 'putting away childish things' would be invoked, and the boys' play would be dismissed in favour of getting down to the serious business of work/learning. In place of the difficult *Star Wars* book that is beyond the children's capacity to 'read', they would prefer that the boys were taught to read from a reader, carefully designed and crafted to appeal to young children of their age and capabilities. Increasingly, the time for this putting away of childish things ('pretend reading') comes earlier and earlier in children's lives. In some cultures, it is not unheard of for four-year-old children to complete hours of homework, after school. What Ivan and his two friends are doing might fall into the category of art and craft, which should be relegated to a later time in the day, when 'work' is completed, and in the interests of including a reasonable balance of work and play in young children's days at school.

The two sides of the fun/work divide, as simply presented above, appear to provide room for easy solutions to resolve issues of teaching and learning. Early childhood educators align themselves with one side or the other. Either they line up at the fun end, and take up a siege mentality, staunchly defending young children's right to play. Or, we put much effort into pointing out the work/learning that is contained in the play. In the first case, we insist that learning can be fun, and there is time enough later for children to knuckle down with drills and skills. We even turn to places like the Scandinavian countries, and champion the fact that children there do not begin formal schooling until they are seven and eight years old . . . and they still learn to read and write! In the alternative position, we insist that the children are playing, having fun, and 'they don't even realize it, but they are learning.' And we list and document this serious work – the boys are prereading, prewriting, measuring, calculating, problem solving. In addition, they are learning the important principles of democracy – individual freedom, choice, negotiating with and respecting others, and so on. Any early childhood text book, or curriculum document, will provide a comprehensive list that could be mapped onto what the boys are doing, in order to 'prove' they are not 'just playing around'.

But this fun/work divide is not so simple, and, in fact, each of the arguments described above actually works to reinforce the divide. In order to provide quality experiences for young children, it is important to examine this divide, and how it works to shape teachers' decision making, and young children's experiences. In fact, it is Ivan who actually messes up this neat divide, and, like the boy in the folktale of the Emperor's New Clothes, pulls the teacher up in her blind acceptance of taken-for-granted beliefs that are a product of her training.

Making it better

If early childhood educators are to resist the academic push-down effect from schools, and maintain play as a key pedagogy in their settings, then they must be able to call on a depth of understanding and analysis. Reliance on slogans and mantras about fun and play actually works to reinforce the divide, rather than disrupt it. In this section, with the help of Ivan's words, we trouble the fun factor, and suggest new ways of thinking and speaking play that will enable teachers to ensure high-equity/high-quality education for all young children in their care.

The teacher's practice is shaped by the theories of developmentally appropriate practice (DAP) (Bredekamp and Copple 1997; Copple and Bredekamp 2009), ideas of democracy and freedom and choice, and beliefs in the importance of play in young children's lives. She has provided a physical and emotional environment that enables play. Time, space, and resources all send the message that children can explore their own ideas, be active and playful, and have fun. There are apparently very few rules, and the children are free to choose what they do, and where, and how, and with whom. At the same time, she can point to the boys' reading, writing, painting, talking, listening to each other, as well as caring and sharing. It should be noted here that, as Ailwood (2003) maintains, the boys would not necessarily name what they are doing as 'play'. The presence of the teacher, and the location of the activity, makes this activity different from what they would be doing, say, in the playground at lunchtime, or at their homes after school (more about this in Chapter 3). Nevertheless, early childhood theorists would consider that the teacher's image of the child is as competent and capable, as she is encouraging their independence at an early age, and permits their use of a book aimed at much older children, and leaves them plenty of time for exploration, experimentation and discovery learning.

But is she really positioning the children as competent, or is it the fun factor that overrides the other discourses? When Robert has apparently been disrespectful about Ivan's efforts, does the discourse of the caring, nurturing mother figure override the image of the competent child? Is the disguising of learning as fun a trick played on the competent child? It would appear that the teacher's first concern on hearing this is for Ivan's self-esteem. She immediately uses this as a teachable moment – to teach the children about the words and actions that are appropriate in a democratic society. Her reaction in turn, causes Robert to look aghast because it is apparent that he has broken one of the invisible rules. She sets about teaching the children about the importance of praise and encouragement, presumably out of concern for potential damage to Ivan's self-esteem. The presumption here, of course, is that self-esteem is built through praise and encouragement, not criticism, even if the criticism is constructive.

But Ivan is having none of this. Instead of Robert's critique acting to destroy the fun, or make Ivan sad, he is adamant: '*it made me want to make it better.*' Ivan is onto the trick about disguising learning as fun and play. This is not his version of fun. Fun, for him, is in the striving, the challenge, and the achievement – like the beauty and aesthetic pleasure and joy from the building of a sandcastle. It is Ivan who reminds the teacher of the purpose here – outcomes, learning, getting better at something. The understanding of fun and play as frivolous, unimportant, and without purpose or goal is not for Ivan. What would make it fun, and learning, would be if someone would help him to make the cardboard box look more like a Pod, and less like a box that the teacher is insisting is a wonderful Star Wars Pod. The work for the teacher here is to provide Ivan with the skills, knowledge and techniques he needs in order to achieve his objective.

Reflections

With the current emphasis on accountability, testing, national standards, and outcomes, many Early Childhood (EC) programmes are eschewing play for more 'work/academic' approaches to teaching and learning. But they come unstuck when they find themselves arguing for the very thing they are purporting to resist. In a recent empirical study conducted in Australia, evidence-based research indicated that some children, in their preschool year, actually knew less at the end of the year than they did when they started (Thorpe et al. 2004). This research understandably angered many early childhood educators, and they rightly put up arguments that questioned the findings. The battle continues. What if, instead of fiercely defending one side of this argument or the other, we start with the premise that there are truths in both of these positions?

What if the teacher is right, and her training tells her that Ivan is much happier learning this way, and would be missing out on the fun if he were to be made to sit down and learn to read through drills and repetitive exercises? Of course, this is painting the worst scenario, and the teacher could reach a compromise through designing play-like activities like word games and Bingo competitions that let the children have fun while they learn, but more serious fun. But in that case, what if Ivan is right, and there is actually more fun (deep fun?) to be had, if only the teacher would take him more seriously, and help him to get better at his play/learning?

It is the role of the teacher that is important here. New times call for new ways of thinking about education. Part of Sutton-Smith's (1997) analysis of play links the nature of schooling to what is happening in the wider society. In agrarian cultures, young children play alongside their parents, and learn through mastering the tools and implements that they will grow up to use in order to make their living. In industrial societies, schools were designed along the lines of factories, with timetables, the division of work from play, and activities prescribed and overseen by 'the boss', who has a vested interest in the outcomes/productivity. In technocratic and post-industrial societies, young children seldom see their parents' workplaces, and more responsibility falls on the teachers to prepare children for their adult lives. But others insist that this is a difficult task, since the children of today will grow up to work in jobs that have not yet been invented. What is the work of the teacher then? To teach the work ethic, or the play ethic?

When teachers focus on the 'fun' without the 'work', they can adapt a *laissez-faire* approach to children's play. That is, they see their role as the 'director', not the 'teacher'. They plan the environment, they facilitate the activities through the resources and spaces they provide, and leave the children the time to play. This assumption is a misreading of the 'learning-through-play' ideas promoted by Dewey, Froebel and others. Instead, it is a romantic presumption that if the children are having fun and playing, they are learning. In the next chapter, we explore these ideas further.

Language shapes our ways of thinking and acting. The fun/work binary can work as a separating device, and when play is seen as the opposite of work, a number of issues arise for EC educators. Too much talk of fun is risky – '*they don't look like they're having a lot of fun.*' And too much talk of work is antithetical to beliefs about ourselves, and what makes us healthy and happy. But this is not a simple matter of whether the teacher chooses play or work. Some teachers put play above all else in their classrooms, and refuse pedagogies that they consider spoiling for young children – such as worksheets, teacher-directed activities, formal instruction or modelling. At the other end of the spectrum, some teachers place importance on more formal instruction and planned activities, perhaps banishing play to the 'free play' category, and children can do this when they have finished their 'work'. And between these two extremes, some teachers struggle to find 'a balance', by including time for play and time for work in their programming.

The art and craft of early childhood teaching is in making decisions about fun, play and work. And it is this crafting that distinguishes the professional from the baby-sitter, parent or child minder. This chapter finishes with some questions designed to provoke further thinking about 'learning through play', and the many ways of thinking and speaking early childhood education and care.

Reflection point

About you

- What is fun for you?
- What do you play? How? When? Where? Why?
- What theories of fun and play sit best with the play in your life?

About teaching

- How would you respond to Ivan?
- How would you assess his learning?
- How would you report on Ivan's learning – to his parents, to other teachers?
- What theories shape your responses to these questions?
- What other theories might add to your thoughts on Ivan?

Practical activities

- Write an advocacy piece for parents, extolling the value of fun and play in their children's lives.
- Write a letter to the editor complaining about play-based curriculum.
- Design a way of reporting on play that maintains the integrity of a programme that celebrates both fun and learning.

Further reading

Ailwood, J. (2003) Governing early childhood education through play, *Contemporary Issues in Early Childhood*, 4(3): 286–99.

Kane, P. (2004) *The Play Ethic: A Manifesto for a Different Way of Living*. London: Macmillan.

3 Naturally produced play

Lulu was watching a group of three girls playing out the story of Cinderella in the home corner. Fiona, the teacher, noticed Lulu at the edge of their game, but it appeared they were excluding her. Fiona took Lulu by the hand and walked her over to the girls. She explained: 'Lulu would really like to play with you. Can she join in your Cinderella game?' The three girls quickly exchanged glances and then responded to Fiona, telling her that Lulu could play.

All the children (first grade) were engaged in various play activities for over 45 minutes. Fiona moved from group to group, observed, made notes, and sometimes stayed with some children. She regularly scoped the room, and everyone appeared to be having fun, busy, and playing. She glanced over to the girls' game a number of times, but did not go near them. She was satisfied that Lulu remained in the game with the girls.

At the end of the session, when it came time for the 'review' of their morning's activities, Fiona asked the girls about their game. The three girls excitedly recounted their game of 'Cinderella'. The teacher asked who played each of the characters, and they listed who was the Prince, Cinderella, the Fairy Godmother, and so on. Lulu was silent, and was not named as playing a character. Fiona asked:

'Who did Lulu play in your game?' The girls quickly glanced at each other again, and one girl explained while the others looked at the floor: 'Lulu was the piece of paper that was in front of the fireplace, collecting the cinders.' Lulu nodded.

When you read this story of Lulu, how did you react? Some readers will be shocked, angry, surprised, and concerned for Lulu. How could children so young be so mean? Others will smile and shake their heads over the innocence and naivety of the three girls. They're just being children. They don't mean it. They don't know any better. Either way, it is the discourse of 'natural' that comes into play here, shaping how we think and speak about the children. Being natural has generally come to be equated with things wholesome, healthy and good. This way of thinking has us striving to live our lives as a close approximation of the way nature intended. When we preserve children's 'pure and natural' ways (James, Jenks and Prout 1998), this is as much about our ideas about our own 'human nature', and our desires. At the same time, we also know that nature brings earthquakes and tsunamis, and these are beyond our control. In this case, the natural brings risks, and we take steps to guard against the danger, control the chaos, or at least minimize the damage. We do the same with 'untamed' children. Teachers' practices are shaped by both these (and other) ways of seeing children and childhoods (James, Jenks and Prout 1998). The trouble with the idea that play is children's natural way of learning is that ideas about what is natural in children are selective. They are a conglomeration of science, tradition, history, culture, and other ideas. And they vary across time and place.

Chapter goals

In this chapter, we examine the idea that play is children's natural way of learning, but we do not spend much time in the arguments over 'nature or nurture'. Rather, we ask different questions. How does the 'natural' discourse work to shape our practices – for better or worse? What does a theory about children's natural behaviours enable us to do in early childhood settings? And what is the trouble with this way of thinking? What does this theory not allow us to do?

- First, we briefly discuss the 'natural' discourse, and how a particular logic works to shape the ways we think about ourselves, as much as young children.
- We analyse the story of Lulu above, and use a number of stories from our observations and experiences in early childhood settings, that unsettle and untidy some of the everyday beliefs and practices in early childhood education that are built on understandings of so called 'natural' play.
- The chapter provides some provocations that trouble ideas of play as children's natural way of learning, and considers how early childhood teachers might use play-based learning as a means of ensuring success for all the children in their care.

Why natural?

In part, how a society views and treats young children says a lot about all members of that society. Our beliefs about children are entwined with our beliefs about our own human nature, and our hopes and desires for the type of people we want to be. The desire to ensure a 'perfect childhood' for the young in our society is tied up with our hopes for the future, in a perfect world. Just as current fears about climate change and the health of the Earth have produced renewed zeal for preserving the planet's dwindling natural forests and resources, so too there is zeal to preserve 'natural' childhoods. Fears about the 'disappearance of childhood' are not new, and are discussed at length elsewhere (see, for example, Postman 1994 and James, Jencks and Prout 1998).

Recently, *The Australian* ran a front-page campaign strongly criticizing a draft new national framework for early years education. The critique objected strongly to suggestions that young children's play involved games of power, gender, bias and exclusion. The newspaper would have none of this, insisting that children be allowed to be children, without imposing political agendas on something that was simply and naturally child's play. This same newspaper regularly raises concerns over school bullying. Presumably, at some age/stage, the child's play ceases to be innocent and playful, and changes into bullying. Education is political, and it would seem that we have a lot invested in the notion of a natural, carefree and playful childhood.

In his keynote address to the 2009 European Early Childhood Education Research Association (EECERA) conference, Michel Vandenbroek (2009) introduced a word of caution for those who will extend their role as early childhood educators to saving the world. We want to believe that young children are carefree, happy, innocent and pure. Of course, there is some truth in this, and young children are vulnerable and in need of protection. However, this can become mixed up with nostalgia for the way we were, as well as fears for 'what has become of the human race'. If we rely on our own partial and incomplete memories of our childhoods, we can romanticize them as golden days, forgetting large chunks of our daily existence as children, and forgetting that not all children have access to such halcyon days, if indeed, they ever existed.

Psychologists have conducted forensic investigation of the childhoods of prisoners, locating early incidents in their 'life stories' that 'explain' their later criminal behaviours. The location of evidence of childhoods and behaviours (e.g. cruelty to small animals) that are not natural, and that are risky and dangerous, points then to later pathologies. 'In depth' interviews and biographies almost always probe celebrities' childhood, for clues to their later achievements (or crimes). Interest in these details is a search for comfort about our own 'normality' and reassures us against the potential dangers of 'human nature'. In Foucault's terms, these technologies of self (1988) produce beliefs in the power of the early years to shape our futures and destinies, and they reinforce our desires for ensuring normal, healthy wholesome childhoods for our young. Emphasis on the importance of the early years works for better and worse in shaping our practices in early childhood settings.

There is a strong history, in many branches of the sciences, of coupling understandings about nature with understandings about our own human nature. Scientificity (Foucault 2000) lends a powerful sense of truth to many of our ways of seeing and thinking. Charles Darwin's work provided a sense of order for our understandings of the world and our lives. His ideas about the survival of the fittest have been drawn on to explain any number of human events, and this theory grew from his close observations of the diversity of life forms on the Galapagos Islands. Freud used the iceberg as a powerful and effective visual metaphor to convey his theories of the subconscious – the part of our minds that is not visible, but believed to be under the surface, and integral to the whole. Skinner kept chickens in his basement to observe their behaviours. What he learned of chicken's behaviour he then transferred to theories about (human) learning processes and thereby education. More recently, studies conducted on fruit flies have drawn conclusions about sleep deprivation and learning and behaviour in humans. Science provides us with systems for ordering and understanding the world. There is presumed to be a level of satisfaction in imposing order on chaos. We think and speak about animals, plants, and people acting or behaving 'naturally', or 'normally' – as nature intended. It is difficult to imagine the commonalities between fruit flies and humans, but we leave this question at this point, and move to discuss the power and effects of metaphors that are used to explain complexities and concepts.

Two powerful metaphors come to mind, for capturing an approach to teaching and learning that builds on ideas about children learning naturally, through play. The first is discussed by Sutton-Smith (1997) and is the delightful image of baby lion cubs frolicking in the grass and sunlight, tumbling, playful, carefree and safe from danger, and yet under the watchful eye of the mother lion. If this image is transferred onto our ideas about young children, we can see their behaviour as playful, and the natural way to develop, all the while practising the skills needed later for survival/life. This image helps to capture our expectations of children's behaviour and development, and the role of the teacher, as well as the curriculum.

But the trouble with this is that, along with what teachers can do, based on this understanding of the natural, come a number of other ideas that this image does not allow. For instance, the presumption here is that learning occurs naturally, without thinking, as if by instinct. There is no place here for direct instruction. This caution against too much teaching, too early, certainly has merit, and the idea of learning naturally through play might fit with the observations of lion cubs at their natural play (ignoring the occasional cuff delivered by the mother lion). But history and culture, along with science, help to shape this idea. This model for teaching and learning may well have been sufficient for agrarian cultures (Sutton-Smith 1997). Children played alongside the adults, using the tools that they would later grow up to use in order to make their living. But in industrial, postindustrial and technological societies, young children rarely enter their parents' workplaces, and their play is no longer directly connected to their later occupations.

The second metaphor goes back to Froebel (1900) who created the name *kindergarten*, which literally translates as 'children's garden'. In many countries, the word is used to describe young children's early years in education. Much has been written about this metaphor (see Weber 1984), and it works as a useful frame for understanding children as natural and, perhaps more so, for understanding the role of the teacher in this site. The work of the gardener varies. Sometimes, she tends the plants, feeding and nurturing, observing, recording, sometimes displaying, and always delighting. Sometimes the gardener has to tame nature, by eliminating the unwanted weeds, applying constraints, selecting, changing and rearranging. The idea of enabling children to bloom naturally under the nurturing care of the gardener is attractive for framing our work with young children.

The trouble with the garden metaphor is the omniscient role of the gardener, who controls the conditions for success. Gardens are stylized versions of nature, influenced by any number of factors – for instance, matters of class, culture, experience, architecture, and community expectations can all shape the 'nature' of the garden. Indeed, gardens are not even possible in some cultures and circumstances. For instance, for so called 'suitcase refugees', who have left their homes with all they own carried in a suitcase, the ability to keep a garden indicates a particular status. A life in camps or constantly on the move does not allow for cultivating plants. Growing flowers and vegetables require stability and a degree of permanent residence. In this case, in addition to the idea of a garden being so much about nature, the idea of the garden is entangled with issues of social and cultural capital. Gardens can be a sign of class and social status.

There is no mistaking that, in contemporary developed countries, 'natural' sells. 'Natural' makes us think better of ourselves and, apparently, look better. Women's magazines devote pages to the benefits of expensive products that help women apply makeup that looks 'natural' (at a cost). Natural food is better than processed food, and here 'natural' means organic. 'Natural' medicines and 'natural' drugs are better for us (not including natural poisonous mushrooms). We are urged to use and consume natural flavouring, natural yogurt, natural gas, bottles of natural water. This gets tricky. For instance, what is natural clothing, and what of nudity?

For the most part, coupling the word 'natural' with other terms generally puts them in a positive light. Natural has come to mean wholesome, healthy and good. Anxious parents worry over their children's temper tantrums, until they can be reassured that they are natural or normal. Being sad can be natural, but being depressed is not. When it comes to clarifying children's natural ways of learning, this is not a simple matter. A conglomeration of ideas from science, religions, traditions, history, economics and other fields, sometimes combine or compete to construct ideas of what is natural. These ideas can be selectively called upon, to powerful effect, for the purposes of regulation and control.

Early childhood educators firstly, through their training, intrinsic values, and any number of other discourses, come to understand particular play as children's 'natural' way of learning. They then set about teaching the children to play in this 'natural' way. Their assessment and evaluation of children's performance is guided by how successfully children demonstrate this 'natural' learning. The belief that the best way to support children's learning and development is through facilitating their play is part of a circular logic. This can be likened to the Ouroborus, an ancient symbol dating back to Plato, who described a serpent or dragon swallowing its own tail. The trouble with this is the presumption that, firstly children are actually learning (naturally) when they play and, secondly, presumptions are made about *what* they are naturally learning.

In the next section of this chapter, we zoom in on Fiona, who is Lulu's teacher in the story at the beginning of this chapter. A regime of truth (Foucault 1988) that insists that teachers plan, act and assess according to beliefs about a universal and natural way of learning (play), enables some children to succeed but also permits others, like Lulu, to be excluded, and denied the same chances for success. It is the work of the teacher, not nature, which controls the conditions for success.

Natural learning: or doing natural

When asked about her classroom, Lulu's teacher explains:

> As far as the children are concerned, they are just playing. I am aware of the curriculum and what they need to learn. They are not aware of this. They are free to choose what they want to play. I observe closely, and I pick up on what they are naturally interested in, and I plan the curriculum around these things. I follow, you know, the emergent curriculum.

Firstly, are the children the players, or the played? (*They are not aware of this.*) Fiona's classroom is a delightful environment, filled with children who all appear to be happy, busy, active and playful. She is a fierce advocate for play-based learning. But this is not simply a matter of the gardener feeding the plants as they grow naturally, nor the lion cubs learning through instinct.

There are many voices at the table. Fiona's approach to curriculum is a product of her training.

Traces of Dewey's progressivism have created an expectation of a room full of happy, busy children (Tyler 1993), engaged in hands-on activity. Ideas of freedom and democratic principles insist on children being *free to choose*. But questions of freedom and choice are tricky. Cultural valuing of independence at an early age leads Fiona to make judgments about their choice-making. Fiona remarked that it sometimes takes until September (nine months in her classroom) before some children learn to choose. She speaks of 'freeing them up'. The children are neither free, nor 'in chains' – they are unfree. There are rules (mostly not spelled out) about what they can choose – and what they *must* choose. Sitting down and doing nothing is not a choice available to them. Fiona designs an environment that acts to produce a particular way of being for the children. The children are not confined to individual desks and are free to move around the room, sit with their friends, play at tables or on the floor, and select from the resources stored on open shelves and within their reach. They can choose to play with blocks, or paint, draw, build with Lego and other similar sets, play in a home corner equipped with a range of kitchen utensils, use magnifying glasses and other scientific equipment, and countless other commercial and recycled materials. The children are encouraged to be active and engage in hands-on activities, talk with each other and Fiona, and generally enjoy themselves when they are in the classroom.

There are those who suggest that the provision of an array of attractive resources might work to produce children as consumers who, as adults, will come to expect and demand the range of choices and array of products when they shop at a supermarket (Cook 2004). In any case, the resources available and the types of play permitted are cultural clues. Toy makers can act as dynamic catalysts of cultural change (Sutton-Smith 1997), with a new plaything spreading quickly throughout a global culture of childhood. Long traditions and prevailing theories shape the type of resources available in Fiona's setting.

When Fiona refers to her observations of what the children *are naturally interested in*, she draws on the principles of the *emergent curriculum*, and the underlying framework of developmentally appropriate practice (DAP). Fiona sets up a physical and emotional environment that tells the children it is OK to play in this setting. There are a number of regulatory techniques that Fiona calls upon to teach the children the type of play that is OK – such as questioning techniques, praise, rewards and reinforcements. Her DAP training has her making notes on her observations of children at their natural play. She makes judgments about her planning and decision making, based on her analysis of these notes. And her understandings about what is appropriate and normal behaviour for these children, at their particular age and stage of development, guide her analysis. Like mice in laboratories, children's natural play is closely watched and monitored.

If children's play in early childhood settings was simply 'in accordance with nature', like the lion cubs, why then does it differ from country to country, city to city, and centre to centre, and even from outside to inside?

On another occasion, Fiona had read the children the story of The Little Red Hen, and the children were all engaged in various follow-up tasks: drawing pictures of the hen, acting out the story, playing with puppets, making 'bread' with playdough, reading recipes for bread, re-reading the story. Thomas, a boy from the classroom next door, was passing by the room on his way to the toilets. He knocked politely on the door and asked if he could please have a word with his friend Darryl. Darryl left his play with chickens and had a brief conversation with Thomas, and then quickly returned to his Little Red Hen game.

When the researcher asked Darryl about the conversation with Thomas, Darryl said: 'We are playing under the tree after we've finished our lunch, and I am up for tiggy.' Even within Fiona's classroom culture, there are a number of ways of seeing play. Thomas is organizing an entirely different sort of play for the lunch break. Which is the natural play? Fiona does not take any observations of the children's play at lunch break, and does not appear to consider what the children do in that time and space to be of interest to her pedagogy.

Fiona accepts folktales as something in which children are naturally interested, and leaves the girls to play out the story of Cinderella. Folktales have historically been used as pedagogy. All cultures have stories that warn children about stranger danger, obedience, fear of monsters, and so on. According to Davies (1993) these tales reflect the ideology of the culture, and work to establish the heteronormativity of the society's expectations. The lessons contained in folktales are important, because failure to behave according to social or cultural expectations can cause distress in individuals. What did the girls naturally learn through this play? Later, in Chapter 5, we take up these ideas in more detail. For now, we stay with the ideas around a curriculum that builds on beliefs about play as children's natural way of learning.

The trouble is that the lesson contained in the Cinderella story was perhaps not the main point here. Is playing Cinderella natural, or is it better conceived of as traditional, or historical, or pedagogical? And is it natural for young children to exclude others? Lulu's experience is disturbing. Is Lulu an exception, or is this too an example of natural play? Is this Darwin's survival of the fittest? If so, what is the role for the teacher here?

Fiona's curriculum approach teaches performativity, and both the teacher and the children are complicit in producing a particular version of play. The teacher provides the environment, resources, guidance, structure. This work of the teacher controls the conditions for success. Those children, who do not play 'naturally' in the environment and with the resources available, are taught to play in this particular way, so that Fiona can feel confident that they are learning. In a number of ways, Fiona's play-based curriculum is exemplary. The trouble is that it is not simply natural play, rather, it is manufactured. And, as evidenced by Lulu's experience, the idea of a classroom full of happy, healthy, wholesome children, learning naturally through play, does not account for all that goes on, nor does it guarantee all children's opportunities for success.

The natural discourse helps shape Fiona's curriculum approach. It also acts on teacher identity. In the following section, we examine how ideas about natural and play come together to produce ways of seeing the early childhood educator.

Teacher as mother

Just as society has much invested in ideas of natural childhoods, it is also important to the natural 'order of things' that we understand mothers as behaving in particular ways. We speak of Mother Nature and Mother Earth, and being in the arms of a loving mother suggests peace, safety, and security. Paintings, poetry, music and literature have all celebrated ideas of a loving, caring and nurturing mother who loves her child unconditionally. Disruptions to this image of the mother either strike fear for the 'human race', or provoke powerful moments of humour (the idea being ridiculous and laughable). The major religions revere the mother, and psychologists, beginning with Freud, place great store in the mother/child relationship, and the power of attachment.

In the field of early childhood education and care, this mother role is transferred to the carer, who stands in for the mother, and replicates this 'natural' way of being. The good early childhood educator is naturally kind and caring, nurturing, gentle, calm and constant. A mother's/teacher's love and approval are considered important to an individual's self-esteem, and a good mother/teacher naturally and unconditionally loves and accepts all that children do.

This ideal is a comfort to those who leave their very young children in the care of another, but Valerie Walkerdine (1984) calls this an 'impossible fiction'. This discursive construction of teacher identity not only produces feelings of guilt when the teacher cannot fit this mould but also constrains the possibilities for the teacher. Can early childhood educators love each child in their care like their mothers do? And what of the male carer? There is no other option available to him. He must also prove himself to be a nurturing, caring mother figure (Sumsion 2000). And what are the archetypes and stereotypes that shape this image? Not the working mother who is sometimes tired, harassed, hurried, cranky and impatient. Not the single mother. Not even the socially active mother who might prefer the company of adults to children.

Our critique here is not a questioning of the role of mothers, either animal or human. But when such a powerful discursive construction is so dominant and pervasive, and it is coupled with the identity of the early childhood educator, it is important to consider how this discourse works to shape our practices.

Three children (aged 3–4 years) were walking around the room with backpacks on their backs from home corner. They moved to a corner area at the back of the room which had a large cushion, and was somewhat obscured by a bookshelf. The children stayed in the corner for 2–3 minutes and then a teacher, Melinda, walked over towards them. Noticing the children were in the corner, the teacher said: 'Out of the corner please. What are you doing over there? What have you got?' Melinda moved over to the corner, directing individual children to move away from the space. She picked up one of the backpacks and looked inside, pulling out three crayons. She said:

> You have crayons in here; crayons don't leave the drawing table. Look, you have drawn on the wall there with the crayons. Move away now please. What will Miss Rachael [group leader was on tea break] say about drawing on the wall? You know we don't draw on walls with crayons. You have made Miss Rachael very sad.

In this setting, as in Fiona's classroom, the children are both free and unfree. They are free to move around and make choices about their play. But they are not free to choose to draw on the walls, or indeed, to move crayons from the drawing table. The teacher too is unfree. She is constrained by the regime of truth that insists that, even when the children are recalcitrant, there are 'rules' for her response. In this case, Melinda does not even express her own negative feelings, deflecting that instead to Miss Rachael, who is not present. It is difficult to imagine that drawing on the walls would make Miss Rachael sad – more likely angry, cross, or, at the very least, annoyed. But an all caring, loving mother does not feel angry towards her child. It is psychology that delivers the punishment. This becomes not a simple matter of actions in need of correction – the children are held responsible for Miss Rachael's happiness. Melinda, the teacher who is actually interacting, does not refer to her own feelings at all (she is most likely concerned that Miss Rachael will find her wanting, in her management of the children). There are no words or actions available to her to express this with the young children.

The children learn quickly about this ever present, ever patient mother figure, and it is probable that some children can scarcely believe their good fortune. Their teacher is certainly not like any adult they have as yet encountered.

> On the first day of school for Year One, Rebecca and Jasmine were playing with a puzzle on the floor. They had not met before this day, but were getting to know each other through playing together. The teacher was occupied on the other side of the room. Rebecca turned to Jasmine and said in a slightly disbelieving tone: 'Watch this. When I call the teacher, she comes . . . TEACHER?' The teacher answered immediately, and started

> walking over. The two girls raised their eyebrows and exchanged knowing looks.

The teacher's regime of truth about being the ever-present, all-caring and nurturing mother figure has positioned her in a way that is going to keep her very busy in the coming weeks and months. In their first day at school, the two girls have learned about their power, which comes from the teacher's view of them and herself.

Finally, this natural mother identity disallows the notion of the teacher as a professional, with training, qualifications, credentials, and accountability. Issues of salary and recognition as professionals are not helped by a discourse that paints the role of the early childhood educator as something that, like mothering, supposedly requires nothing more than what nature provided.

In the way of the Ouroborus, a curriculum design and approach that insists that children learn naturally through play, and are overseen by a teacher who strives to approximate a mother figure who is naturally loving, caring and nurturing, works to produce a child who acts according to a manu-factured version of the natural – a child with natural flavouring, perhaps! In the last section of this chapter we take up two natural interests of children that rarely feature in the manufactured natural child.

Manufacturing the natural child

We cannot leave a discussion about children's natural ways of learning through play without raising the most obvious, and yet frequently overlooked, natural thing about children – their bodies. When schools refer to the 'student body', the concern is with students' minds, not their bodies (Butler 2005). This way of seeing children begins in the early years. Even though nappy changing, and later toileting, are carried out as part of everyday routines in order to meet the natural needs of young children, the bodies of young children are nevertheless considered risky sites. Privacy for young children in early childhood settings is rare (Giugni 2008). Any play connected with this aspect of learning requires surveillance. It is generally a requirement of the architecture of early child-hood settings that toilets have transparent partitions, enabling full vision. This enables teachers to offer any assistance when needed but also to be vigilant for any risky play that might develop in that space. Their natural body functions, along with their natural play, are constantly observed and assessed.

There is at once recognition of children's natural interest in their bodies, and a suspicion of the potential risk involved. Sutton-Smith refers to a cat-egory of children's play that romantics do not care to acknowledge. He calls it the phantasmagoria of children's play – their fascination with the dark side, horror and gore. Along with this, we would place their playfulness and curios-ity about their bodies, and their sexuality. When it comes to young children's

natural ways of learning, through curiosity and playfulness, there are parts of
the body that are, in the main, strictly off limits in early childhood settings. A
cursory glance at any of the wall charts in early childhood settings designed
to teach about the body will show that instruction in this area is more a matter
of geography than biology (Johnson 2000). Here again, it is a conglomeration
of history, culture, tradition, mixed with a dash of Puritanism, that has produced this way of seeing children. This most natural of interests in their own
bodies must be reconstituted into a version that is 'civilized', or better yet,
ignored. Mostly, children learn this quickly, and yet they continue to explore,
surreptitiously, and 'under the radar' of the teacher.

> Yonnie (aged 4.5 years) is playing with three other girls in the home
> corner. There is no adult present, except for our researcher who is operat-
> ing a hand held camera, and recording the children's play in this area.
> Yonnie carefully places a length of material over the play sink, part of the
> regular equipment in such a home corner, a scaled down version of the
> kitchen sink, with wooden taps and a bench. But Yonnie has other ideas
> for the sink. She climbs up and sits across the sink, facing outwards to the
> other girls, with her legs hanging over the front. And she proceeds to
> make loud and repetitive 'farting' noises by blowing raspberries through
> her mouth, much to the amusement of the other girls. After quickly
> checking the researcher's reactions (she makes no response, and con-
> tinues to film), Yonnie continues with the noises, and the other girls gig-
> gle and laugh, while nervously watching for the researcher's response.

We suspect that this play would not have occurred if the teacher had
been present. Presumably, part of Yonnie's delight was in her awareness
that her behaviour was transgressive. The rules about this natural interest can
vary. Conceivably, farting and other body noises are a perfectly acceptable
source of humour in Yonnie's family home, or are considered natural – as
nature intended. Natural, yes, but not acceptable. It serves children well to
learn the social mores. (For further analysis of this vignette, see Chapter 5.)

Sexuality is another contentious issue in the early years. On the one hand
there is the very real risk to vulnerable children from the actions of paedo-
philes. However, a rising moral panic around young children and sexuality
runs alongside the increasing sexualization of children at younger and younger
ages – at the hands of the media, consumer marketing, and popular culture. In
her 2005 study, Blaise followed the play of young children (aged 4.5 years)
in an urban kindergarten, and showed how they used their understandings
of heterosexuality to play out and regulate the gendered social order of the
classroom. The girls talked a lot about make-up and how they used make-up to
'get boyfriends' (Blaise 2005: 95). Some of the children were classified as fashion girls (who always had boyfriends), and fashion guys, and according to one
of the boys, Alan, 'fashionable means sexy' (Blaise 2005: 96). These children,

according to Blaise's analysis, were playing out their understandings about gender and heterosexuality. However, too much talk of sexuality, and body functions and noises, will generally trouble ideas of children's natural learning through play. If indeed these issues are directly addressed, either with the children, or in the teachers' training, they are usually in relation to child-protection programmes, and cause for being alert, if not alarmed.

The morally dominant forms of right and proper behaviour take precedence over ideas about natural learning and play. For the most part, orthodox early childhood practices manufacture a version of the natural child, who is good, wholesome and healthy. Any departures from this culturally mediated version of natural play draw the concern of the teacher. Children should be naturally happy, active, busy.

In one setting, we observed a child, Elsa (aged 4.5), who was happy and busy, in her own company. We saw her singing, acting out stories, and engaging with toys and other objects, for the purpose of self-amusement. Elsa was aware of others around her and joined in their play when she chose. Elsa's teachers described her as 'shy', 'a little strange' and 'having difficulty engaging with others in play'. The term 'solitary' was used often to describe Elsa.

In early childhood settings, 'natural' is a category, unspoken, but constituted and mediated through social interactions, traditions, cultural norms, interventions and daily practices. Words like 'strange', 'shy' and 'solitary' signal 'not natural'.

Reflection

Caring for 'nature' is important to the health of our planet, and the way that a society cares for its young children is a measure of the health of that society. But we began this chapter with a caution against a misguided zeal for preserving a version of childhood that is built on a mixture of science, tradition, history, nostalgia, and culture. The belief that early childhood educators can 'save the world' through producing the natural child has driven many EC reforms. A misreading of approaches such as 'whole-language' literacy education, can reduce the role of the teacher to 'facilitator', overseeing children as they learn naturally through play. The teachers' beliefs are shaped not simply by things natural but by theories of teaching and learning that claim to replicate nature, while insisting on certain ways of thinking, speaking and acting. The trouble with this is that when children's cultural, community or family values and practices do not fit with the teacher's ideas of what constitutes children's natural way of learning, through play, these children can be observed, scrutinized, and found wanting. Their chances for success are dependent on the conditions made available to them by the teacher.

About you

- How much do you remember of your childhood?
- Are your memories mediated through artefacts, other people, popular culture, other devices?

- What is your earliest memory of a lesson you learned in your childhood? How did you learn it? What did you learn?

About teaching

- How would you respond to the three girls who played Cinderella?
- How would children in Fiona's classroom stand the best chance of success?
- What theories shape your responses to these questions?
- What other theories might add to your thoughts on Lulu's experience in the Cinderella game?

Practical activities

- Devise a metaphor that could account for your approach to teaching and learning.
- Write a response to the national newspaper that campaigned against the notions that young children's play included issues of power relationships, injustices, and sexuality.
- Build on Fiona's approach to curriculum so that it might take into account a wider spectrum of playful possibilities.

Further reading

Blaise, M. (2005) A feminist poststructuralist study of children doing gender, *Early Childhood Research Quarterly*, 20: 85–108.

Davies, B. (1993) *Shards of Glass. Children Reading and Writing Beyond Gendered Identities*. Sydney: Allen & Unwin.

Sumsion, J. (2000) Oppositional discourses: deconstructing responses to investigations of male early childhood educators, *Contemporary Issues in Early Childhood*, 1(3): 259–75.

4 The glamour of play
Play as serious business

In early childhood education there are long traditions of both play and art, and a book about play cannot ignore the arts. Any number of taken-for-granted beliefs about children and their education sit comfortably across both play and the arts – ideas about creativity, imagination, freedom, self-expression. Creativity is enjoying particular currency, having shifted from the exclusive domain of the arts, to business, industry and even economics (see, for example, Florida 2003; Pink 2005). But theories of creativity can be loosely applied and, as Claxton (2002) proposes, used to describe the ordinary and the mundane. Teachers can talk about children's natural creativity when all that children are required to do is stick cotton tails on templates of bunnies – 'bunny-bum art' (McArdle 2003).

In this chapter, we focus on the arts for a particular purpose. The collapsing of play with art is contestable on a number of levels, but we leave that discussion for other places and people (for more on this, see for example, Wright 2003, 2007; McArdle 2008). In this chapter, we consider some of the beliefs and practices in the arts in early childhood as a means to illustrate 'trouble with play'. Some of the points might just as well apply to any of the other 'disciplines' – literacy, numeracy, science – and some are unique to the arts. Our analysis in this chapter is framed by questions of what art does, and how regimes of truth about art work to shape play pedagogies in early childhood settings. In particular, we consider how the image of the competent child both enables and constrains. We note the growing trend towards documenting and publishing glossy, full colour and expensive books, which feature beautiful, artful photographs of children at play and children's artworks. We raise some questions around how this appears to be glamorizing and commodifying play, and turning the documentation of play into a serious business (an economic concern – a serious way of fund raising).

Chapter goals

- We examine play/creativity/arts as a site where particular discourses come together, sometimes colliding and competing.
- We discuss how art works to shape ideas and practices – about the competent child and play.
- We finish this chapter with a case study that illustrates how one approach to early childhood arts education was played out with pre-service teachers, working with young children and their family day care contexts, and how dominant discourses about play prevail in the activity.
- Finally, we provide some provocations around ways of seeing art as play, and the role of the teacher in making children and their learning visible.

What does art do?

Every year it seems, newpapers run stories about some animal making art. One year, in our particular regional newspaper, there was a story about the dolphins at Seaworld producing paintings. Another time it was elephants in Burma. In 2006, in the Sunday paper for our State (Queensland, Australia), *The Sunday Mail*, it was a Cocker Spaniel named Zoe, and the article featured a photograph of Zoe making paintings on canvas, with a 'specially adapted brush in her teeth'. The header for the article was 'Paw-casso!'

When interviewed, Zoe's 'mother' (owner) explained that the paintings were popular gifts for all their friends:

> Zoe loves painting. It only took a couple of months to teach her . . . she just loves learning. The first painting she did was a present for another dog, but the others I have given to people or kept to hang on my wall. She's also painted Christmas cards for my friends and family. They could hardly believe she'd really done them . . . I think most animals could probably paint if they had the right teacher.
>
> (*Sunday Mail*, 12 March 2006, p. 28)

The trouble with this is that it can be very similar to what happens in many early childhood settings. The activities in which children are engaged are not much different from Zoe's achievements (outcomes?). There is a false grandiosity about what Zoe is doing (Paw-casso!), and false explanations attached to what could simply be described as a gimmick. In early childhood settings, for

Figure 4.1   Zoe and her specially adapted brush.

much of the time, when children are 'learning through play', we suggest that nothing more than what Zoe is doing is expected of the children. Young children are provided with 'specially adapted' tools (large paint brushes, scaled-down furniture) and learn to perform painting, and to produce something 'cute' that can be displayed on the refrigerator, and given as gifts. The photograph in the paper of Zoe, and the words spoken by her 'mother' could just as well form part of teachers' documentation and observations of young children: Zoe [Nelson] holds the brush in her mouth [his right hand], dips it in the red paint, makes large downward strokes onto the canvas . . . and so on.

Our questions here are not whether Zoe is having fun, nor whether she is playing or working, nor whether she is happy, busy, healthy or 'normal'. Rather, it is the gimmick factor that attracts the attention. It is less likely that photographers rush to take pictures of young children painting at easels, put them in the newspaper, and marvel over what they are doing – although that does happen! We wonder whether Zoe engaged in the same process that absorbed the likes of Picasso (as suggested by the article's header 'Paw-casso!' – exclamation mark included). Or is this just a gimmick that Zoe has learned to do, albeit through training? Does the provision of a canvas add glamour to the exercise?

More importantly, of course, we wonder how decisions are made about what children are doing when they paint? Is it enough that they are having fun, busy, happy, and producing bright colourful artworks? Or should there be more to what we expect of them, and what they expect of art? The questions here for early childhood educators are about purpose, intent, and the expectations we have of young children.

In most early childhood settings today, you will see displays of children's artworks on the walls, and around the buildings. We suggest that this is a practice that, like others we have discussed in previous chapters, has been shaped by a conglomeration of tradition, history, culture and community expectations. What purpose does this serve, and what expectations does this practice create? Is it read as evidence of the children having fun? Learning naturally through play? The teacher is 'doing' developmentally appropriate practice? Is doing art simply equated with playing? What do children learn about art when simply left to play, like Zoe?

Reflection point 4.1

Consider the following list of possible explanations for the taken-for-granted practices in the arts in early childhood. (We go on in this chapter to expand on some of the issues raised in this list.) How do you respond to the points raised here, and how do these practices shape the work of the teacher and the image of the child?

- Children's artworks are 'naturally' colourful and bright, and they provide schools with 'a look' (see Bresler 1993; McArdle 2008), indicating happy, healthy children.
- Art provides a 'window to the soul' (see Hubbard 1994), and provides teachers with access to children's thoughts.
- Art is a language, and a means for communication, when words are not available, or inadequate (Wright 2003).
- What do you think Zoe's 'mother' means when she says: 'if they have the right teacher'?

Practical activities

- Watch the newspapers and other media over the following months, and make notes on how the arts are positioned in your culture and community.
- Make a list of the benefits of play. Make a second list of the benefits of the arts. Compare the two lists, and reflect on how they shape your understandings of the role of the teacher in early childhood education.
- Discuss the newspaper story of Zoe, and reflect on the implications this has for the work of early childhood educators. What are the implications that might be drawn about their work, and what is missing from this picture?

Glamour added

The story of Zoe the wonder dog is a story that is played out in early childhood settings daily. Children are provided with specially adapted resources, and encouraged to play. Their paintings and drawings have a special appeal, but they are invited to play at any number of activities. The 'good' early childhood teacher closely observes the children at their play, documenting, either by noting observations or taking digital photographs. With digital technologies becoming increasingly accessible, photography can be used to record more detail of children's play, and photographs can be displayed just as easily as children's artwork. Documenting children's play has become a serious business, in more ways than one.

> A colleague of ours, a sociologist, recently talked with us expressing his dismay with his parent/teacher interview, reporting on his son's performance at kindergarten. When we asked about his concerns, he explained:

>> They had a dossier on Nelson (aged 4 years) that was this big [exaggerating, but indicating a file that was 15 cm high!]. I reckon they have recorded every word Nelson has ever spoken, every thought he might have had, and every little scribble he has made on paper. Why do they watch him so closely, and write down every single thing he says. What's that about?

Nelson's teacher takes portfolios seriously. Documenting children's play has become a serious business. While an early childhood practitioner might read this story above as evidence of a quality programme, the benefits and purpose of Nelson's 'dossier' are lost on his father (and quite possibly, on Nelson). His use of the term 'dossier' suggests something more sinister than the terms that have come to be more commonly used in early childhood settings, such as portfolio or documentation.

In the early twentieth century, Maria Montessori (1870–1952) developed a teaching system that was radical at the time, blurring the distinction between learning and playing. Her methods remain influential in various models for early childhood education still today. Montessori considered young children's artworks as meaningless scribble, and warned against putting children's artworks up for display (see Montessori 1965). According to her methods, children were to be taught art appreciation and aesthetics, as well as skills and techniques for developing their artistry. Now, at the turn of the twenty-first century, another radical method emanating from Italy has wide-reaching influence around the globe – a method that was the original conception of Loris Malaguzzi (1920–94), and has come to be referred to in shorthand as the

'Reggio Emilia approach' (see Edwards, Gandini and Forman 1998). This approach is based on an image of the child as competent and capable, with rights as well as needs. The play activities and artworks produced by children in these centres are reproduced in international exhibitions and glossy publications, and they are celebrated and analysed.

When it comes to the arts, these are two very different approaches, emanating for the same culture, but almost a century apart. Our colleague in the story that began this section has never heard of Reggio Emilia, but we feel safe in presuming that Nelson's teacher has. The documentation of children's play, their words and their drawings, has become a taken-for-granted practice that is read as an indicator of quality practice in early childhood education. Observations have traditionally been considered an essential component of pedagogy and the planning cycle in early childhood education and care. But the Reggio people have taken this to a new level, turning it into what, in some senses, is an art form (see for example, *Reggio Tutta*). The Reggio term, 'documentation', has been taken up internationally, and prescribed in many curriculum documents and accreditation standards around the globe. From Montessori's opinion of 'meaningless scribbles', children's art (and play) is now taken seriously, documented, analysed, and exhibited. The competent child has been made visible through artful documentation, and to powerful effect.

The trouble with this is connected with Nelson's father's comment above. Documentation can enable and constrain teachers' work. It can enable children's learning and capacities to be made visible, and enrich teachers' planning and pedagogy. But, we know of many early childhood teachers who now spend many hours preparing portfolios and increasingly glossy and glamorous displays of children's activity. If there is an expectation that this information is shared more widely with others, taking the form of the glamorous publications that seem to have become connected with 'doing Reggio', then it is documentation as product, rather than process, which takes precedence. Nelson's father puzzled over the gloss and the detail of things that he frankly thought of as everyday and mundane parts of Nelson's existence. As well as having very little interest in what he saw as the minutiae of Nelson's day, his father also considered the 'dossier' an intrusion, and he expressed dismay at what appeared to him to be an unnecessary level of detail, suggesting surveillance.

The elevation of children's art from meaningless scribbles and children's play to the subject of photography and the object of close scrutiny has worked to reshape the image of the child. Rich and glossy images celebrate the competent child and the beauty in the minutiae of everyday occurrences. These public displays of the children's achievements can work to create a self-consciousness in the children, and in some cases we know of, children stop what they are doing in order to inform their teacher that they might want to photograph or write down what they are about to do. It seems that it is not the play that is important here but the business of recording the play.

A number of developments in the arts have also led to increased awareness and appreciation of young children's competence and creativity. This relatively recent view of the competent child has led to children's art reaching the wider community, beyond the classroom. Some art galleries have made space for the display of young children's artworks, framed and labelled. One way to look at this is to see the positive shift towards viewing children as citizens, competent, and with rights as well as needs. Their artworks can provide a window to their lives, and make them visible in the wider world.

It might also be said to reinforce a trend to commodify children's art as product, even beyond the range of gifts for doting grandparents and relatives. Children's art sells, or even approximations of children's art. Their drawings are used as 'decoration' for anything from dinner plates to Web sites, presumably denoting playfulness, innocence and naivety, fun. At the Olympic Games held in Sydney, Australia, in the year 2000, children's artworks adorned the walls of rooms in the athlete's village, and souvenir mugs and other artefacts featured young children's artworks. In commercial terms, they are a cheap and readily available resource. Teachers and parents are complicit in this commodification, with the growing practice of exhibitions of children's art in kindergartens as fundraisers, sometimes even auctioning each child's work, to be sold to the highest bidder.

At the risk of seeming churlish in our critique of a practice that has seen children made visible and celebrated rather than dismissed, we raise one more point that troubles us about the glamorizing of children's art. Logic suggests that it would be in the interests of the market to keep children (and their art) at a certain level of development that makes it attractive. Here we are referring to the 'cute' factor. What sells here is the 'other-ness' of young children – unsophisticated, uninhibited, unknowing, untaught. It is the delightful 'stick figures', wobbly arms and legs, bright and colourful splotches of paint, and purple trees that appeal. It is the children's 'mistakes' or 'deficiencies' that are actually considered charming. The role for the teacher is diminished when there is an insistence on a certain type of children's (perhaps 'natural'?) attempts in the arts. And the competent child comes to mean the child who does not need to learn anything more. But what of the child who becomes unsatisfied with this 'childish' style and wants to develop more skills and techniques? This child who wants to become more competent has nowhere to go with this version of pedagogy. And what of the child whose family, community or cultural values have produced a very different idea of the form/purpose for art? That child has to learn the 'rules' of 'school art'.

This glamorizing of what amounts to very early and exploratory experiences with paint, crayons, clay and so on, is not just about art. In much of the documentation that appears on classroom walls, or in glossy publications, the artfulness can be said to be in the photography. And the subject matter in the photography is just as likely to be the children at play, not necessarily with the arts. Documentation can feature a series of photographs, for instance, following children as they walk down the stairs, or as they leaf through a book, or as they stand on the sidelines watching other children play. That is not to say that teachers' observations of any of these examples are not important, and there may be very good reasons for watching children so closely. The trouble is with the idea that documentation, in whatever form, needs to be displayed artfully, and if indeed needs to be recorded at all in some cases. If the serious business for the teacher becomes the process of documenting, rather than interacting, guiding, modelling, or teaching, then we wonder, like Nelson's father: What's that about?

In the next section, the mystery, we consider how the shift came about, from seeing 'meaningless scribbles' to 'Picasso' in children's art, and how this shapes what and how we teach young children about the arts, and what and how they learn. The idea of the competent child, who is producing work similar to Picasso, has appeal, especially to a teacher who knows little about art, and therefore does not know what or how to teach it.

Reflection point 4.2

- How do you assist children to develop artistically? How do you assist them to learn to read, write, speak? How do you help them develop mathematically? Consider the similarities and differences in your responses.
- With the *laissez-faire* approach, which children will have a better chance of success? And which children will be excluded or disadvantaged?
- Do you think the insistence that children learn naturally through play celebrates the competent child, or reinforces the 'otherness' of young children?

Practical activities

- Select six examples of artworks by young children (either children you work with, or find some on the internet). Record your analysis of their work, and what it tells you about the child. Does their artwork provide a window to their thinking?
- Interview six children, and ask them about their views on art. Record their responses, and arrange them into categories.
- Make a list of ten famous artists, and as many of their works as you can name. How many of them are indigenous to your country? What are the implications for your arts programme with young children, depending on how you completed this list?

The mystery

A recent study conducted with children aged 4–5 years in both Hong Kong and Australia (see McArdle and Wong 2009) asked the children 'What is art for?' In this phenomenological study, one of the intriguing categories was that children considered art 'a mystery'. The mystery was that the teacher made them do art, it was a daily activity, and she taught them how to do it . . . and yet, art was not something that adults, or even older children in school, did. So it was apparently important when you are in preschool, but not important in any other context. Nobody else appears to value art – it is just something that happens in the kindergarten.

It could be said that there are a number of 'mysteries' about the arts. Just as with other big discourses, like religion and play, the arts are the site of institutionalized contradictions and ambiguities. Art can attract millions of dollars in the auction room, and be dismissed as valueless rubbish by the general populace (Berger 1982). There are those who insist that it is art for art's sake that is important to the human race, while others value art for life's sake. And the art/Art, and creativity/Creativity debates continue. The question 'what is art?' can be counted on to stimulate a robust discussion in many walks of life.

Like play, the arts can be a powerful culture clue. For instance, we would have very little knowledge about the ancient Egyptians and their culture, if it weren't for their arts (Wright 2003). Australia has a shameful history of the treatment of its indigenous peoples, a history that many Australians were never taught in schools. But recently, and significantly through the arts (music, dance, drama, media and visual arts), more Australians have come to be aware of that black history, as well as coming to appreciate the rich cultural dimension of the Aboriginal and Torres Strait Islands peoples. The arts made a major contribution to this shift, and the moves towards reconciliation. Celebrations, festivals and rituals are all important cultural and societal events. They are outside and above the everyday, or 'real life' but they reinforce the power and identity of the community.

The arts are like play, making a risky space where dissent and subversion are permitted (to a degree), and where 'normal' societal expectations and structures can be disrupted and resisted. Historically, the *carnivale* (Bakhtin 1981) provided a space where the clowns and the jesters were able to protest playfully, using the arts to question and resist the order and structure of the ruling hierarchies. Employees of Google are encouraged to spend a portion of their working week at 'play', working on projects that are a departure from their everyday duties, in the belief that in this space, new ideas emerge. Artists have always wanted to make people see things differently, and avant-garde artists aim to disturb the cultural and societal norms. The arts, and play, provide not only space for communication, but also for thinking.

We suggest there are mysteries about play. There are those who see its importance and value, others who dismiss it as worthless. Anthropologists have studied children's play activities as indicators of cultural norms and traditions. And play is a site where risk, imagination and departures from 'real life' are permitted (within reason), accepted and even sometimes celebrated. When children 'play school' or play 'mothers and fathers' they sometimes hold a mirror to our practices, and prompt new ways for us to see how we work with children. Or they seize the opportunity, in play, to try out new ways of being, through magic and fantasy. In play, children develop their own culture, and it is a space where they can subvert and resist the regimes that govern them. The romance of the Disney version of children's play sits alongside the Brothers Grimm, and play can be a site where children gambol in the sunlight like the baby lion cubs (see Chapter 3), and/or a site of regressive, oppositional and illicit power (for more on this, see Chapter 6).

Finally in this section, we raise one more mystery in the arts – the pedagogy and the play. If artistry and creativity are something all young children 'naturally' do, why then do we meet so many older people who firmly maintain that 'I don't have an artistic bone in my body', or 'I couldn't paint a picture to save myself'? What happens to the natural 'talent'? Is it not taught enough, or taught too much? After 12 years of schooling, it is common for students to enrol in their first year of university studies, and have to learn how to draw – architects, engineers, doctors, nurses, teachers, designers, and many more trades and professions require skills and abilities in drawing. It would seem that the arts are the real space where teachers do expect children to learn naturally through play. But this leads us to repeat the questions that we raised earlier. How and what do they learn? And what do teachers expect that they are learning?

In Chapter 3, we used the Ouroborus, the ancient symbol of the snake swallowing its tail, to capture some of the circularities in the production of beliefs and practices in early childhood education. Nowhere is this more apparent than in the arts. Modernist artists, at the turn of the twentieth century, deliberately set about challenging the 'rules' of art. Marcel du Champs drew a moustache on the Mona Lisa, and used a wordplay to suggest she was a whore. His purpose was to disrupt the bogus religiosity (Berger 1982) that surrounds the elite view of art. The modernist artists played with the rules of art, and created new ways of seeing art.

The irony is that a number of the modernists (including Klee and Kandinsky, for instance) turned to young children's artistry for their inspiration (Wright 2003). Picasso is commonly quoted (although his words are frequently misinterpreted) as expressing the desire, as he grew older, to paint more like his grandchildren. And now, play pedagogies in arts education in early childhood produce artworks that approximate these artists' works. As Zoe's 'mother' maintains, they just need 'the right teacher'.

Through praise, encouragement and reward (every child's work is displayed), the children learn that the teacher is pleased when they produce a certain type of painting. Their art is read, analysed and interpreted for evidence of the freedom and self-expression that the modernist artists championed. But this is not the same play. The children are not playing with established rules. Rather, they are unaware of any rules, and their teachers are not indicating that there are any. In the arts, we celebrate children's unschooled work, and then we hear critiques of works that hang in the National gallery: 'My two-year-old could do that!'

Documentation as pedagogy can perpetuate this romance of the child as artist/poet. When children's words are written down and read by others, they may indeed become poetry, and have wisdom attributed to them. But they might just as well be quite simply utterances that once spoken, are forgotten – by the child. Our caution in this chapter is a revisiting and further illustration of one that we have raised in an earlier chapter: are the children the players or the played?

A case study

To finish this chapter, we provide a partial account of a project involving a group of preservice student teachers, and their attempts to put theory into practice, with young children in Family Day Care settings. The case serves to illustrate the power of the dominant discourses of play in early childhood education, and some of the confusions that arise when discourses collide and compete.

The context

The Regional Coordinator of Family Day Care (small groups of young children cared for in the family home of the carer) approached the university with a proposal. She wanted to fund a project that would celebrate the organization's thirtieth anniversary and thought a children's art exhibition would be the appropriate way to mark the occasion. Preservice teachers enrolled in an elective unit in arts education in the early years worked with the children and their carers, with dual goals. Firstly, the students would try out some of their theory in 'real-world' contexts. Secondly, the regional coordinator would have a training resource, for future professional development for carers.

Stage one: planning and preparing

The students worked together at university, preparing quality arts experiences they would provide for a small group of young children (aged between 2 years and 4). They drew on their discipline knowledge about the arts, as well as their developing ideas about quality arts education. In groups of three, they visited their family day care (FDC) setting, and met the children and the carer in her home. At university they shared their observations and information with their teacher – details about the children, the carer, and the environment. Planning was based on the students' understandings of quality arts experiences. They planned to introduce arts vocabulary to the children, and teach them some skills and techniques, depending on the context and the planned activity.

Each group of students selected a different starting point or focus for its activity. Three groups chose an arts element – line, colour, texture. One group chose a medium – clay. At their teacher's insistence, the plans included attention to how the students would assess the children, and evaluate their own teaching. This did not sit comfortably with the students because the idea of assessing young children's art was not something they felt prepared to do.

At university, the students tried out their planned activities themselves, in order to understand the experience, and so that they could anticipate what support the children might need. They also gathered and organized all the materials and resources that they would need, including story books, paint, crayons and pencils, paper, and cameras for recording.

At this point, the students had careful and thoughtful plans for their approach to pedagogy, using play-based strategies for teaching the children about some elementary content in the discipline knowledge of the arts. They were not comfortable with the idea of imposing too much structure and so left parts of their planning open ended, waiting to learn from the children about their interests, which would provide them with more direction.

Stage two: implementation

Students arranged to spend up to two hours with the children and the carer, this being the first of two planned visits. In this first visit, students spent time getting to know the children, introduced the planned activity, and helped the children with their art making.

In this account, we focus on the group who planned to teach the children about line. The children were of mixed ages, Ruby (aged 2 years), Sean and Julia (aged 3 years), Sam and Alyce (aged 4 years). The plan was to read the children a story which would draw their attention to the beauty of the natural environment. Next, they would walk with the children around the garden, looking at lines and shapes and colours in Nature. The students took magnifying glasses and bottles, to prompt the children to look closely, and to collect leaves and sort and categorize them, according to line or shape or colour. Later, the children would draw and paint, and create a group mural, using paints, crayons and collage, on a large sheet of thick brown paper. The students drew from their reading of a wall mural project in Reggio Emilia.

As they went for the nature walk with the children, the students took digital photographs, and made notes about what the children said and did. Sam was looking at one particular leaf and I said: 'Look, this leaf has dots on it. Can you see the spots?'

Sam replied: 'I'm allergic to spots.'

Stage three: reflective practice

After the first visit, all the groups of students returned to campus, to share their experiences, reflect, and plan the follow-up visit. They were surprised by how long everything took, and frustrated that things had not gone according to plan. At this stage in the project, many of the students were disappointed, anxious, frustrated and close to panic. One student was reluctant to return to her FDC setting, and was upset with the carer, and annoyed that her planned activity 'didn't work'. To make things worse, one group, the 'clay group' came back excitedly reporting on the success of their activity.

At this point, the students found certainties and reassurance in returning to the play pedagogy discourses. They wanted to abandon their initial plans, deciding they were too ambitious, or simply that the approach did not work. The clay group's stories of success hinged mainly on their observations that

Figure 4.2 Documenting children's play: glamour and serious business.

the children played happily with the clay for over 40 minutes. The 'line group' heard this and expressed disappointment with their experience, judging it a failure. They had difficulty getting the children's attention. When they read the story, the younger children wandered away. And they felt that the afternoon had been chaotic, with nothing much to show for their efforts. Their ideas of the competent child seemed to have been abandoned quickly, and they all rolled their eyes and made jokes about the children's lack of engagement with the tasks. The question of assessment becomes important here. If the success of pedagogy is judged solely on the children being happy and not making too many demands beyond a manageable level, then the clay group were successful. But there was no discussion about anything to do with the discipline knowledge of the arts, in relation to clay. The point here is not to insist on the serious business of teaching as opposed to play and fun. The question is around the role of the teacher, and how pedagogical approaches are shaped.

The teacher asked the line group students what they would do on their second visit. They immediately decided that they would take clay in their next visit. In the arts education literature, the mystery over the prevalence of 'gimmick art' (Wright 2003) might be partially explained though this case study. Rather than the competent child, there is also a fear that young children have short attention spans, get bored, and then make trouble. In the mistaken belief that their pedagogies did not work and they had failed to engage the children, the line group rushed to change their plans, searching for an alternative that might be of more interest to the children. Ideas about happy children playing overrode any thoughts of teaching discipline knowledge or skills. The objective became to have the children happy and busy – and no trouble!

Their teacher had them revisit their goals and objectives, and their theories about quality arts experiences. She also prompted them to closely analyse the documentation they had made of the children's words and actions. The line group decided (somewhat reluctantly and with only a small measure of confidence) to stay with their original plan but made some adjustments informed by the new knowledge they had acquired about the children and their capacities.

Stage four: return visit to the children

The students in the line group were delighted with their second visit, and pleasantly surprised with their success. When they arrived at the gate, the children ran out to meet them, calling out: 'It's the leaf girls!' Sam ran to get a box of leaves he had been collecting in anticipation of their next visit, and all the children were excitedly talking about leaves. That afternoon, the children worked on the large sheet of brown paper, which the students had laid out on the ground. As the children painted, glued and drew, the students sat with them and talked with them, as well as photographing and recording some of the children's words and actions:

'This one matches. Your shirt is pink too.'

'Ooh! Squiggly!'

'Spiky line.'

Back at the campus, students engaged in some robust discussions about what they had learned, links between theory and practice, what worked and what didn't work, and what they would do differently next time, or when they had graduated.

But there was one final dilemma – the exhibition! The students agreed that most of what the children had produced was unsuitable for framing and presenting in the form of a traditional art exhibition. When they looked at the artworks in this light, much of it was messy, coming unstuck, or 'simply scribble' (Montessori's meaningless scribbles?). Panic again!

Stage five: the exhibition

At this stage, the students and the teacher would have been happy to abandon the idea of the exhibition, and discussed the merits and the richness of their experiences to date – theirs and the children's. However, there was an expectation and an agreement that the exhibition would take place. And it was hugely successful.

With the help of the expertise and resources available through the university graphic designers (and funding), the exhibition consisted of six large A1 glossy laminated posters (see Figure 4.3), which documented the children's work through photographs and the children's own words. The teacher collaborated with the graphic designer, briefing her on the principles and objectives. The teacher selected what was important content, and then the graphic designer organized and arranged the materials artfully. On the night of the exhibition, some artefacts were aesthetically interspersed with the posters, a video of the clay activity played, and a loop of beautiful photographs played over on a projection. The carers who attended the exhibition spoke enthusiastically of the experience, and the coordinator was pleased with the resources available for later use in her planned professional development programmes.

This case study captures a number of the issues that we have raised in this chapter but probably the most interesting for us is the glamour of the exhibition, which showcased a set of beautiful, designer-inspired, glossy posters, which were much admired on the night, and the teacher has received a number of subsequent requests to purchase the set, from practitioners in entirely different cities. It seems to us that the actual substance of the experience, the children's engagement in the arts and play, and the preservice teachers' learning experience, became subsumed by the glamour of the posters and the occasion. While an audience from a range of education contexts admires and

Figure 4.3   Poster.

discusses the posters, we feel fairly confident that the children (and the pre-service teachers) have more than likely moved on and barely remember the experience in the detail that is now shared with others. This is not to say that documenting teaching and learning has not proven to be a powerful professional tool, since teachers are keen to see how other teachers work, and this is nothing new. The trouble with this trend now is the seeming requirement for a level of gloss and glamour, and the exhibitions, and how this business/commodification seems to take precedence over the serious business of teaching and learning. Not every teacher has the resources of a graphic designer to call on!

Reflection point 4.3

- When the teacher reflected on this project she asked 'Did we just *do Reggio*?' What is your response to this?
- Why do you think the line group was so eager to abandon its plans?
- The teacher has presented these posters at conferences, and has been surprised when early childhood teachers approach her afterwards, enquiring about purchasing the posters. What is your response to this?

- What and how do you think the preservice teachers learned through this experience?

Practical activities

- Make a plan for teaching about mathematics through play. How will you determine what the children are learning? When you have assessed the children's learning, what will you do with the information?
- Make an argument for leaving young children to simply learn about art through play, exploration and discovery. Describe what the children will do, and the role of the teacher.
- Now make an argument for children learning to read through play. Describe what the children will do, and the role of the teacher.
- Discuss any similarities and/or differences in the two arguments you have constructed.

Further reading

Knight, L. (2008) Communication and transformation through collaboration: Rethinking drawing activities in early childhood, *Contemporary Issues in Early Childhood*, 9(4): 306–16.

McArdle, F. (2008) The arts and staying cool, *Contemporary Issues in Early Childhood*, 9(4): 365–74.

Woods, E. and Attfield, J. (2005) *Play, Learning and the Early Childhood Curriculum*, 2nd edn. London: Sage.

5 Play rules
Rules for play

Researcher: Who makes the rules up?
John (5.3): Teachers . . . 'cos they're the boss.
Researcher: Do children ever make the rules?
John: No.
Researcher: What happens if you break the rules?
John: You get in trouble.
Researcher: What do you get in trouble for?
John: . . . You get in trouble for hitting, punching, wrestling, play-ing naughty games . . . all sorts of stuff . . . If I get caught I say I don't know [when asked questions]. When I say why, I go to the door. But first if they say that's not good enough [reason], I go to the door. [The child has to sit next to the door, which is the exit to the room.]

Play 'rules' in many early childhood settings. By this we mean that a lot of early childhood settings value play and incorporate it into their everyday activities, calling their programmes play-based and the like. It also seems to mean that play rules as long as adult rules for play are obeyed. This chapter draws on empirical data in the form of vignettes to investigate rules for play (see Chapter 1 for sources of vignettes). We present a range of vignettes as a way of prompting thinking and reflection, and by no means set out to 'cover' the gamut of rules that might be found in early childhood settings. Reflective points as well as practical activities are provided to encourage discussion and contemplation of ideas. The goals for this chapter are to encourage readers to:

- question and analyse rules used in early childhood settings;
- consider who makes the rules, who breaks them and why, and the consequences;
- think about how rules can impact the fairness of play;
- consider democratic principles of play.

Using the vignettes that follow, we raise issues about what it means when 'play rules' and discuss 'rules for play'. We also consider play that might be banned, and provoke readers to think about rules that are unspoken and how children learn them. Our aim is to promote engagement with, discussion of, and reflection on not only adult rules, but also those initiated by children. We tease out some of the ways in which 'play rules' and in which rules for play operate in the complex daily life of classrooms for young children. But first we discuss relations of power.

Rules are one way in which adults are able to adopt positions of power in relation to children. When working in early childhood settings, teachers are located in positions of power and authority because they are acting *in loco parentis*, that is, in place of a parent, or instead of a parent. Teachers are required to take on some of the functions and responsibilities of a parent and act in the best interests of the child as they see fit, as long as civil liberties are not violated. Relationships of power are an integral part of the social relations in which persons engage on a daily basis. Depending on the situation, power relationships can be negotiated, resisted, challenged, contested, endorsed and changed. Power relationships construct ways of thinking, feeling, being and acting, and define what can be said and done in particular social settings. So in early childhood settings adults are enabled by relationships of power to position themselves more powerfully than children. Children are constrained because of who they are (age, size, legal status, and so on) and can therefore be positioned less powerfully than adults, but this does not mean that they are powerless: they have ways and means of resisting and challenging adults. If daily preschool activities are characterized by 'teacher formulated rules, which constitute impediments to children's influence in their everyday lives at preschool' (Arner and Tellgren in Emilson 2007: 15), then it might be expected that children will challenge and resist some rules.

Adult rules for play can be explicit or implicit. Explicit rules are stated regularly by adults and are often common knowledge. In the transcript excerpt opening this chapter, John knows that if you break the rules, you get into trouble. He is also able to name some of the things that get you into trouble, and these are well known by the children in this classroom. Implicit rules are not stated but are assumed to be understandings shared in early childhood settings such as classrooms, in both indoor and outdoor play. Learning the explicit rules can be hard for some children but learning the implicit rules may present more of a challenge. Sometimes adults assume there are shared understandings when there are not. And if adults become aware that shared understandings do not exist, sometimes the rules are stated and then become explicit. At times rules remain a mystery, especially if they relate to the dominant culture and are not explained to children from different ethnic, cultural and social backgrounds. In early childhood settings, explicit rules might include bans on play that:

- uses guns;
- is violent or destructive of property;
- involves anything sexual;
- is too dirty and messy;
- is too loud;
- is too uncontrolled and risky;
- is driven by popular culture (e.g., *Astroboy, Ben 10* etc.);
- is not listed above but could be described as 'naughty'.

Reasons for banning such play could be that it's too risky for staff, in that play could get out of control and children might be hurt. What children think is a different matter completely (see Sandseter 2009). Because of their own values, adults might object to gun play and the violence that is associated with guns. Morally, adults might think that play involving reference to anything sexual is inappropriate (naughty?) for young children and too risky for them to supervise while children are in early childhood settings. This may include role playing 'doctor' and events such as birthing babies. Play that is too dirty or messy or is seen by some as too much trouble to clean up. It can also be seen as chaotic and out of control (see Chapter 4). Dirty, messy play may even be seen as unsuitable for girls. In many contexts, climbing trees and using hammers and nails have succumbed to contemporary risk-averse society and are either rarely seen or are not possible because of the regulations governing what happens in group settings for children (Nordic countries excepted). Teachers are often judged on the amount of noise coming from their classrooms but a quiet environment does not necessarily indicate that more learning is occurring than in a noisy classroom. Playing superheroes has had its fair share of negative commentary: 'Our staff has chosen to limit superhero play. We have banned toy weapons, violent videos and books, superhero costumes, and all aggressive play, even when it is pretend play' (Hampton 2002: 86). Others see it differently, with 'scary war play' being valued as it provides 'a deep release for emotions' (Honig 2007: 78). There is little valid evidence that gun, violent and superhero play is increasing in early childhood classrooms (Boyd 2002). Banning superhero and aggressive play runs the risk of denying children access to powerful learning opportunities and as Boyd suggests, may provide a developmental function that is as yet, not known or understood. To Colker (2008: 70), teachers' willingness to take risks and 'go against the norm' is one of the 12 characteristics of effective early childhood teachers.

History is useful when thinking about why certain types of play might be banned in early childhood settings in contemporary times. As discussed in Chapter 1, some influences in early childhood education date back centuries. One of these is the Christian idea of original sin, which shaped the approaches of many educators and parents in Britain and the USA in the seventeenth and eighteenth centuries, and became known as the Puritan evangelical tradition. It is associated with physical punishment, discipline, strict routines and Christian training to rid children of evil habits (Cleverley and Phillips 1987). Influences of this tradition are evident today: 'Right habits develop when children do what they are told, play orderly games, and are not allowed to play war games or games in which they pretend they are adults or dress up in adults' clothes' (Cleverley and Phillips 1987: 33).

Penny Holland (2003), UK author of *We Don't Play with Guns Here: War, Weapon and Superhero Play in the Early Years* says that banning violent or gun play emerged in the 1960s and 1970s in an effort to reduce the 'spiral of male violence' (p. 8). In hindsight, it seems to be an attempt by zealous teachers at redeeming the situation through peace education. Holland says that it was wrong to assume that preventing boys from playing aggressive games would reduce adult male violence and that there is no evidence to support a link between aggressive childhood games and adult male violence. In fact Holland suggests that it may be counterproductive to stop boys playing aggressive games as they can become disruptive and live up to a 'bad boy' image. This can occur because they are constantly told that their play interests are unacceptable, which conveys messages that they are 'bad' and causes them to seek attention in negative ways. Holland thinks that boys will engage in gun play regardless of attempts by parents, early childhood settings, and schools to stop them. In Holland's study, the majority of nursery schools that relaxed their ban on guns, swords and violent games reported that many boys had more fun together, had enhanced self-esteem, and over time became more creative in other areas of play. Some staff noted that there was less tension because adults were not repeatedly saying 'no' when children wanted to engage in war, weapon or superhero play.

Vignette 5.1: adult rules: banning Barbie dolls

Holland (2003) takes up the issue of girls and Barbie dolls, which were banned in some settings for the simple reason that guns were. However, girls used the dolls that were available at the centre and because their play was 'peaceful and presented no management problems it did not attract the same negative attention as the stereotyped boys' play' (Holland 2003: 24). Holland reasoned that boys involved in gun and aggressive play attracted continued negative attention, which challenged their gender identities and subsequently reduced their self-esteem because their gender wasn't being affirmed. The girls playing dolls, however, 'were receiving general validation for being quiet, settled and cooperative' (Holland 2003: 24). Holland read this as enhancing the self-esteem and gender identities of the girls, which led to more confidence.

Reflection point 5.1

- Why might it be unfair to affirm the actions of girls as quiet and cooperative, and provide negative responses to boys wanting to engage in war, weapon and superhero play?
- There are boys who do not engage in war, weapon and superhero play. If adults are policing potential digressions into gunplay etc., what attention do these boys receive?
- There are girls who like war, weapon and superhero play. What might be the effect on girls if boys are constantly discouraged from this type of play?
- Add your own points . . .

Practical activities: guns and dolls

- Start by making a note of your current ideas about girls and doll play; boys and war, weapon and superhero play; and boys who do not engage in war, weapon and superhero play.
- Make a point of observing girls playing with dolls on five different occasions, noting what they do and say, how they play with the dolls and the type of things that staff members say when they talk together. Record your thoughts and ideas.
- Observe boys engaging in war, weapon and superhero play on five different occasions, noting how they are playing, who is doing and saying what; and what staff members say to them. Record your thoughts and ideas.
- Observe boys who do not engage in war, weapon and superhero play, noting how they are playing, who is doing and saying what; and what staff members say to them. Record your thoughts and ideas.
- Make a table that shows a summary of what was happening each time you observed for each group. Compare and contrast children's actions and words, and staff members' actions and words. Look back at your notes about your current ideas about each of the three groups. Do you still think the same? Identify what you have learned and reflect on it. If your views haven't changed; reflect on why this might be the case.
- Add your own points . . .

Vignette 5.2: the sink-toilet (see also Chapter 3 in relation to the natural child)

Three girls are playing in the home area. Yonnie (4.5) is sitting on the wooden child-sized sink and using it as if it is a toilet. She makes 'farting' noises with her mouth and tongue, laughs and laughs, looking around as she does. She jumps down, and Rebecca approaches with a blanket, which she places over the top of the sink. Rebecca then sat on the blanket, which covered the sink, and as she sat made 'sssshhh-ing' type noises to indicate she was urinating, all the while looking at and smiling at Yonnie. When Rebecca jumped down, she removed the blanket and Yonnie sat on the sink again. Rebecca put the blanket over Yonnie, but Yonnie pushed her away and said 'D-o-n't!' Yonnie remained on the sink, continuing to pretend it was a toilet and began to make farting noises again. Rebecca tried again to cover her with the blanket but Yonnie pushed her away and continued to 'fart'. Two other girls nearby continued playing without becoming involved.

This event occurred in an area that encouraged kitchen and house-type play. In our experience, what these two girls were doing is not unusual as children often 'play around' with everyday bodily functions such as eating, snoring, sleeping and toileting (see Chapter 3 for a discussion about this vignette and natural play). The teachers were not aware of what was happening and so there was no comment about the play or intervention in it. Had they been aware of the play it may have been able to continue as it did, without comment from any adults. Both girls were obviously enjoying themselves because of the way they were laughing and smiling. In classrooms where this type of play is not permitted, there are risks involved. They include the risk of adults seeing and/or hearing the play and other children telling teachers about the play if it is not allowed. Their noticeable enjoyment suggests that if the girls thought it was risky, it was worth the risk.

Reflection point 5.2

- Is this play acceptable? Why? Why not? Discuss reasons that it might and might not be.
- What do you think made the girls enjoy this so much? Discuss what they might have gained from playing this way.
- Consider the idea that many girls have few opportunities to feel powerful. Think about recent experiences where you have felt powerful – what memories do you have of how you felt?
- If this play was risky in the context, then playing this way might

have made the girls feel powerful, especially if the teachers weren't nearby. If it wasn't risky, was it still a way to make them feel powerful? If so, consider why.
- Add your own points . . .

Practical activities: the sink toilet

- Think about what is happening in this vignette and decide what you would do if you came across this type of play. Discuss your view with colleagues (students, teachers).
- Next time you meet a similar situation, remember what you decided you would do and say. Reflect on whether you upheld your view or changed it and said and did something different from what you had decided. Reflect further about why you think this might be the case. What would you do next time?
- Add your own points . . .

Vignette 5.3: pack-away time

The teacher in the 'toddler' room, where children are aged 15 months to 3 years, was sitting on a chair with children on a mat at her feet. The children had just completed tidying the room and the teacher was asking individual children what they had packed away. In a conversation with each child the children told the teacher what they had packed away, and the teacher confirmed that each child had tidied the toys they named. The teacher also commented if she had seen that child tidy other toys as well, in addition to those they mentioned. She then gave each child a sticker, which was placed on their arm, for helping to tidy the room. The children know the rule that they have to tell the teacher what they have tidied so that they can have a sticker. All children except one are attentive and wait patiently for the teacher to name them and then tell what they have tidied.

Reflection point 5.3

- The children know the process and the rules. What might happen if no tidying was completed? Should a sticker be awarded? What are the possible outcomes of not giving a child aged 2 a sticker?
- Contemplate what might happen when the children change rooms

and teachers, and extrinsic rewards are not used in the new classroom. How might this best be handled?

- Stickers are an extrinsic reward, something tangible given for a task undertaken, in this case tidying to the satisfaction of the teacher. Discuss alternatives to using extrinsic rewards for children this age (15 months to 3 years).
- Discuss the advantages and disadvantages of intrinsic motivation with children this age. Consider whether intrinsic motivation could work effectively in this situation with children this age.
- Add your own points . . .

Practical activities: rewards

- Make a list of your views about extrinsic rewards for children aged 0–5 years. Make notes about how they reflect your views of children and childhood. Identify relationships of power evident in what you have written: how are children positioned; how are adults positioned?
- Find a definition of intrinsic motivation from a text book. Read about it and consider how it can relate to children aged birth to five years.
- Discuss intrinsic and extrinsic motivation with other students and/or teachers, sharing ideas from your list.
- After the previous activities, look at your list again and reflect on whether any of your views have changed and why they might or might not have.
- How are adult differences of opinion about intrinsic and extrinsic motivation handled when these differences occur with staff working in the same room?
- Add your own points . . .

Vignette 5.4: Is there anything you can't play here?

Researcher:	Is there anything you can't play here?
Jason:	You can't play guns or *Ben 10* [Ben, aged 10 found a device that could transform him into 10 different alien heroes. *Ben 10* videos, games and Internet downloads are available].
Researcher:	Why do you think that is?
Jason:	Umm, a bit rough.
Researcher:	Who makes the rules?
Jason:	The teachers 'cos they're big. No children make rules. Sometimes they [children] can say what they want to play with.

Researcher: What happens if you're not doing the right thing?
Jason: They go to the babies' room.
Researcher: Is there anything you really want to play but can't here?
Jason: I really want to play *Ben 10*.

This vignette has similarities to the examples discussed by Holland (2003) in terms of the type of play that is banned (guns and *Ben 10*). Jason suspects the reason for not allowing the play is because it can be a bit rough. Two things are of interest here: the first is who makes the rules and the second is the consequence of not abiding by the rules. Like other studies (e.g., Corsaro 1985; Corsaro and Schwartz 1999; Williams 2001; Emilson 2007), the children we talked to from three childcare centres identified adults as making the rules. They also talked about how children deal with adult-imposed rules. Both Jason in this vignette and John (transcript excerpt at the beginning of this chapter) stated that adults make the rules because they're big or the boss. They go further and let us know that no children make the rules. Adult rules apply to groups of children in classrooms and include rules such as no guns. Children do make rules and tend to do so when they are engaged in child-initiated pretend play (see Curran 1999; Pramling Samuelsson and Johansson 2009). In child-initiated pretend play, children are in control and can make rules and choices.

Reflection point 5.4a

- How could children be involved in making rules for the classroom?
- What are the benefits of involving children in making classroom rules?
- What power relationships operate when teachers and children make rules?
- What are the issues associated with involving children in making classroom rules? Discuss democratic processes for involving children in making rules: is co-construction of classroom rules possible? For instance, if children wanted gunplay and teachers didn't, whose ideas might dominate, and what are the implications of this? What about 'policing' the rules? Would some rules be enforced in preference to others, say those favoured by teachers? Is democratic rule making possible in early childhood classrooms?
- Are there equitable ways of teachers and children making and enforcing rules?
- Add your own points . . .

The second point is the consequences of not obeying the rules. Both John (transcript excerpt at the beginning of this chapter) and Jason talk about the consequences of not obeying the rules and both were in no doubt that this leads to trouble. As John said in response to the question about breaking the rules, 'You get in trouble.' Trouble for John was time out, that is, having to 'go to the door' as he said, which meant sitting near the door of the classroom. Trouble for Jason was the indignity of being sent to the babies' room, although it didn't sound like Jason had experienced this as he said '*They* go to the babies' room.' So according to these boys, punishments are used in their classrooms and they are well aware of what they are. In both cases punishment was exclusion from the group, one to the periphery (you have to go to the door) and the other removal from the room altogether, a 'sentence' of time with the babies. Both are punitive.

Perhaps it is teachers who sometimes need time out. Barbara, a teacher in a nursery room who worked with children from birth to the age of two, talked about needing to step away from a situation and reflect on why she was upset. She had been 'battling' unsuccessfully over a few days, trying to get a child to sleep when it all got too much. She said it was her fault, and not the child being a 'trouble' in going to sleep (refer to Chapter 3, for a discussion about teacher as mother/good early childhood educator). Barbara said she should be aware and read the signs in herself about why she was feeling aggravated about not being able to get the child to sleep.

Reflection point 5.4b

- What do children learn from punishments such as 'time out' on the periphery of the group and removal from the group altogether?
- Who is time out for? (See the example of Barbara, above.)
- What are the alternatives to using time out?
- What is the implication of sending children to the babies' room as punishment?
- If a child is excluded from the group and 'timed out', it is highly likely that the adult has seen the child's behaviour as resistant or challenging adult authority. What power relationships are at work when adults use time out in such situations?
- Add your own points . . .

When preschool teacher Anna was asked what happens when children cross boundaries in play, she said that they were given three warnings and if the behaviour continued, a written behaviour report was completed and discussed with the child's parents. She said that the director of the centre might also have a 'chat' with the child as that sometimes helped to improve behaviour, mainly because the director was presented as a person with authority (and was therefore scary?). This all sounds very serious for children aged 4–5 years and is reminiscent of the behaviour policies that most primary (elementary) schools have these days.

Practical activities: is there anything you can't play here?

- In your workplace (staff member) or where you undertake field studies (student), identify the type of play that is discouraged or disallowed. Discuss with a colleague or small group why you agree or disagree with 'the rules'. List other options that could be tried or adopted.
- List the methods of 'punishment' that are used in your workplace (staff member) or where you undertake field studies (student). Discuss with others alternatives that could be tried; or reflect on reasons for staying with what already occurs.
- How are differences of opinion amongst staff members about rules and punishment handled?
- Discuss how rules and punishment could place adults in positions of power in relation to children. How might more equitable power relationships be developed?
- Add your own points . . .

Vignette 5.5: rules for sleeping and waking?

Matthew (1.10) remained asleep while the rest of the children and staff were preparing for afternoon tea. As it was past 3 p.m. the teacher decided to wake Matthew so that he did not 'miss out on afternoon tea' and could 'eat at the same time as the other children.' Matthew was woken and carried to the table where the other children sat waiting for their food to be brought from the trolley. Upon seeing Matthew, Sam (1.11) squealed, and with a broad grin on his face, pointed to Matthew and said 'Matthew wake now, Matthew wake.' Matthew was placed in the chair next to Sam and the staff began to put bibs on each child and place a bowl of yoghurt in front of them. The children began to eat. After two mouthfuls, Sam leaned towards Matthew and kissed him on the cheek. Matthew turned his head toward Sam and smiled. Matthew and Sam then began to eat again.

Being past 3 p.m. is important in the decision to wake Matthew. The reasons given by the teacher were in the interests of Matthew not missing the important event of afternoon tea and not having to eat alone if he woke later. As it turned out, waking Matthew and seating him next to Sam resulted in a special moment being shared between Sam and Matthew. We don't know whether waking children who sleep past 3 p.m. is an explicit rule or not in this room, or if it is, whether it is adhered to rigidly. It could be a parental request. But on this day it was something that the teacher decided to do and brought delight from Sam and reciprocated pleasure from Matthew.

Reflection point 5.5

- Should there be rules for sleeping and waking? Why? Why not?
- What are the advantages and disadvantages of having set rules about sleeping and waking times for children?
- What are the advantages and disadvantages of having a flexible approach to sleeping and waking?
- What is the role of parents in decisions about their children sleeping and waking while in early childhood settings?
- What are the implications of rules being bent or broken? For example, letting children sleep longer than their parents want; waking up children because they have slept too long but this results in a very upset child for a long period of time; waking up children to eat, play or go to the toilet . . .
- Add your own points . . .

Practical activities: sleeping and waking

- List the rules for sleeping and waking that you have seen in a centre (or that you use yourself).
- Ask several other students or teachers to do the same thing.
- When complete, share ideas and discuss each point, taking care to discuss fully, noting reasons for rules, and similarities and differences between rules. Discuss reasons for differences. Identify where power relationships might be at work in rules (refer to explanations of power relationships earlier in this chapter).
- Identify and reflect on how differences in opinion amongst staff members; and between staff members and parents about sleeping and waking are handled.
- Rewrite your list and compare with your first attempt. Date this list and do the same thing 6 months and 1 year later, and then at regular intervals, noting changes and reflecting on them.
- Add your own points . . .

Vignette 5.6: 'good girl eating all your fruit'

Staff were removing children's lunch boxes from the fridge. As they took out each lunch box and placed it on a spare chair at the table, the child it belonged to was asked to come and sit at the table. Natalie (2.9) was called over to the table. She picked up her lunch box and began looking through it, picking up items and turning them over in her hand. She selected a piece of fruit and closed her hand around it. She looked up and sat with the fruit in her hand, watching what the teachers were doing at the fridge. When both teachers were looking into the fridge, Natalie left her chair at the table and put her fruit in the rubbish bin. She returned to the table, and looked over her right shoulder in the direction of the teachers as she sat in the chair. Natalie continued to sit and watch what the teachers were doing. When one teacher went into the bathroom and the other was bending over the next table opening children's yoghurt containers, Natalie picked up the two pieces of fruit remaining in her lunch box, left her chair and placed them in the bin. As Natalie returned to the table, she looked over her right shoulder in the direction of the teachers. Natalie took three biscuits from her lunch box and placed them in the bowl in front of her. She then began to eat the biscuits. As the teacher moved to the table where Natalie sat, she looked at each of the children's bowls and when she got to Natalie said 'Good girl [for] eating up Natalie.' The teacher then looked in Natalie's lunch box and said 'Good girl eating all your fruit too Natalie.'

Natalie managed to deposit three pieces of fruit in the rubbish bin without staff noticing. Other children may have seen what Natalie did (or not) but no one mentioned it to the teacher. Being busy, the teacher must have assumed that Natalie ate all the fruit, but she may not have known that Natalie had three pieces. Her comment suggests she knew that Natalie had more than one piece. As this scenario happened within 3–4 minutes, it would have been very difficult for Natalie to eat three pieces of fruit in this time. In the busy-ness of making sure all children got their lunch boxes, it escaped the teacher's notice that it was unlikely that Natalie could have eaten three pieces of fruit in this space of time. The rule here seems to be that Natalie should eat all the fruit in her lunch box. Not only has she disposed of three pieces of fruit deliberately and unnoticed, but she was also praised by the teacher for eating, and shortly after, for eating all her fruit (a subtext here is that good girls comply by eating, and eating all their fruit: eating makes a good girl). It is unlikely that the fruit would be found in the bin as it was covered with a lid that swung backward and forward when rubbish was deposited. Unless the teachers were to search the bin, they would not know that the fruit was there as it was concealed by the lid.

In early childhood settings, children do things that adults do not see and hear, or know about; and adults do things that children do not see and hear, or know about. There is no way that we can realistically see, hear or know everything that happens. Some children try very hard to make sure adults do not see certain things. While what Natalie did involved no other children, there are occasions when children's actions have significant effects on others. The point is that while we can do nothing about things that we do not know about, there are occasions when actions such as Natalie's are observed by staff or children; and children may or may not tell staff what has happened. In this case, if the teachers had seen Natalie, would it have meant that she was no longer a 'good girl': would she have been a 'naughty' girl? The reflection point for this vignette is therefore about what might happen if staff had observed Natalie's actions.

Reflection point 5.6

- What would you have done if you had observed Natalie's actions? Why?
- Consider the idea that Natalie may have positioned herself powerfully by secretly putting the fruit in the bin and defying the expectation that it was to be eaten. This was something she alone knew and could make her feel very powerful.
- Think about how Natalie might have felt when she was praised for eating the fruit after throwing it in the bin.
- What similar experiences have you had, what did you do and why?
- Add your own points . . .

Practical activity: 'good girl eating all your fruit'

- With colleagues recall similar experiences you have had in your work or as a student. Explain what you did and why. Discuss different ways of handling the situations and the advantages and disadvantages of each.
- Add your own points . . .

Vignette 5.7: who drew on the table?

Seb (2.9) is intent on finding out who drew on the table, asking both children and an adult if they had done the drawing. At one point Seb appeared to implicate Jane (2.9), who in turn denied strongly through words and facial expressions that she had drawn on the table. Seb showed acute awareness about rules related to drawing on furniture. He adopted an authoritarian role in pointing out the issue, admonishing those around him, directly accusing Natalie and pointing with his finger to add emphasis. Natalie defended her innocence and continued to play as she had been. Seb also demonstrated responsibility for addressing the problem by trying to remove the drawing with a plate that he rubbed repeatedly over the top of the table.

What Seb said and did indicated his understanding of the violation that had occurred. Contrary to other examples of children informing teachers when rules have been broken (e.g., Pramling Samuelsson and Johansson 2009), Seb took personal responsibility for trying to remedy the situation by attempting to find the culprit and to remove the drawing. He was successful with neither.

Reflection point 5.7

- What might be happening here? Is Seb placing himself in the role of teacher when he attempts to find who is responsible? How might it make him feel to behave this way?
- What of those around him who were accused? How might they feel?
- What action would you take in response and why?
- Add your own points . . .

Vignette 5.8: Natasha

Natasha (4.1) was concentrating hard, her face contorted and red. She was gripping the child-sized rectangular table with both hands and had the upper part of one leg and a knee resting on the table. The other leg supported her while she made repeated pelvic thrusts against the corner of the table. The teacher saw her and said nothing (this was not the first time it had occurred). Other children saw what she was doing but they seemed oblivious, asking her to come and play. Natasha said she would be there in a minute. She continued for several more minutes before joining her friends.

Reflection point 5.8

- If you were the teacher, what would you do? Why?
- Would you talk to Natasha's parents? Why? Why not?
- What do child development books say about masturbation in relation to girls and boys? What do you think about this?
- Is masturbation by girls more 'taboo' than boys? Why? Why not?
- Add your own points . . .

Conclusion

Ostensibly, play rules if the rules of play are obeyed. The nature of some rules has been shown in this chapter using vignettes and other examples. These rules relate to everyday occurrences in classroom life and because of that may seem too mundane to be of any significance. However, rules are at the heart of what happens in early childhood classrooms and are templates for what gets challenged and negotiated; the ebb and flow of what plays out in the complexity of daily life in early childhood contexts. Rules are also value laden and culturally specific, as are the early childhood settings we create and the decisions made by teachers on a minute-by-minute basis.

Further reading

Pramling Samuelsson, I., and Johansson, E. (2009) Why do children involve teachers in their play and learning, *European Early Childhood Education Research Journal*, 17(1): 77–94.

Sandseter, E H.S. (2009). Children's expressions of exhilaration and fear in risky play, *Contemporary Issues in Early Childhood*, 10(2): 92–106.

Rewards

Reineke, J., Sonsteng, K. and Gartrell, D. (2008) Nurturing mastery motivation: no need for rewards, *Young Children*, 63(6): 89: 93–7.

Shiller, V.M. and O'Flynn, J.C. (2008) Using rewards in the early childhood classroom: a reexamination of the issues, *Young Children*, 63(6): 88–93.

6 Fair play
Playing fair

Much play in early childhood settings reproduces the status quo. That is, it reproduces what exists in society in terms of relations of power about 'race'; gender; social, economic and cultural capital; ethnicity; heteronormativity, and proficiency with English. Through such play, children can be marginalized and isolated for any of these reasons, combinations of them, and more, including size, age and skin colour. The focus on educational play has worked to conceal how children use play to position themselves more powerfully at the expense of others (Sutton-Smith 1997). Various studies show how power is used overtly and covertly in 'free' play to marginalize and isolate children through physical and verbal means, often in collusion with others (Walkerdine 1981; Danby and Baker 1998; Brooker 2002; Mundine and Giugni 2006). But it doesn't have to be this way. Learning about how marginalization happens provides ways of addressing bias and unfairness that occurs in play. In this chapter we prompt readers to think about what constitutes 'fair play', and what 'playing fair' means in the everyday life of early childhood classrooms.

From what is known about children's play, 'free' play times are when it is most likely that injustice will prevail. We are not suggesting that all free play is laced with unfairness and prejudice, simply that it has been documented as occurring at these times. Free play is extended time for pretend play that is mostly child initiated. Historically, there is little adult involvement in pretend play as children rarely make contact with teachers when 'they are engaged in play or other activities chosen by themselves' (Pramling Samuelsson and Johansson 2009: 88). The amount of free play that occurs depends on the teachers, the curriculum, and the location of the centre. Free play in the Nordic sense means play that is 'free from excessive adult control, oversupervision, and interference' (Wagner 2006: 293). In contrast to the Nordic countries, Wagner (2006: 293) described free play in the USA as something where

> . . . adults have specified a brief time, say 15 to 30 minutes, in the pre-established daily schedule when children *are allowed* to do what they

want to do, often *if* they have finished the tasks the adults have given them. In many settings, especially in the kindergarten and primary grades, children earn the right to play on Friday afternoons if they have behaved nicely and complete their work on Monday through Thursday.

There is wide variation in early childhood programmes and it is highly likely that the type of programmes found in the Nordic countries also exist in the USA. However, less time for free play does not eliminate discriminatory behaviour.

Globalization has brought changes to the cultural and ethnic composition of many nations through immigration, the Internet, and global economic policies and franchises. Wars in various places have also produced an unprecedented number of refugees and asylum seekers who are resettled in new countries through the United Nations. The treatment of new migrants and refugees has become more salient since terrorist events in the early years of the twenty-first century (e.g., 9/11), as have concerns with rising xenophobia, the place and status of indigenous peoples and the need to address racism. According to Siraj-Blatchford (1994: 22), 'Racism is embedded in the very fabric of our society and is largely hidden.' Many young children know that 'white' skin is preferable to any other skin type (MacNaughton and Davis 2001; Mundine and Giugni 2006). Many migrants and refugees experience racism, as do indigenous peoples. For instance, in the UK, 'older phenotypic notions of "race" have survived in the popular imagination, as well as among some policy makers' (Rutter 2005: 10). Rutter (2005: 10) cites the British National Party as continuing to promulgate 'ideas of distinct races, racial separation and repatriation of those who are not white.' The USA has a long history of immigration (including slavery) and, as Nieto and Bode (2008: 7) note, immigration is one of the 'most contentious issues' in the country. In Australia, addressing racism has attracted increased media attention and assumed heightened significance since the Sydney 'race' riots in December 2005. Some of the Nordic countries have recently experienced a change in the composition of their population with the arrival of refugees and immigrants. In Denmark, for instance, migrants now constitute 4.1 per cent of the population and in Norway it is 3 per cent; while in Finland there are over 100 different migrant groups, with most coming from Russia and Somalia (Organization for Economic Co-operation and Development (OECD) 2006). For early childhood educators, these population changes mean greater diversity in the classroom.

With children from a wide range of ethnic and cultural backgrounds in early childhood classrooms comes responsibility to teach for diversity and difference. However, this responsibility is just as great for teachers working with children and families where there is less diversity, that is, where homogeneity or monoculturalism prevails. To teach for diversity and difference, teachers must move beyond romantic ideas of children as innocent, naïve and incapable of being discriminatory, making racist comments or marginalizing others. In other words, children learn about power relationships at very young ages and can be just as influential in perpetuating racism, classism, sexism, heteronormativity and so on, as those who are older. Discriminatory and biased values and beliefs are 'taught', often implicitly and unknowingly.

This chapter draws on a range of data to show how children's play perpetuates the status quo, how it reinforces social and cultural divisions and strengthens those who are already in more powerful positions. For those working with young children it is important to learn to see the ways children include, exclude and marginalize, and to act to interrupt the perpetuation of injustice. Play is value laden and culturally specific, as are the programmes provided for young children in early childhood settings and the decisions that teachers make. Young children's 'play' can include teasing, bullying, cruel jokes and tricks, racist beliefs and practices, sexism, and games that are unfair, unkind, and isolating. Staff may be unaware of such events; or if they are aware, have few strategies for handling such situations in equitable ways to ensure that all maintain respect and that children are not subjected to discriminatory acts. These examples are used to make a case for:

- teachers to know and understand that play can reproduce unjust and inequitable circumstances;
- teachers and children to know what fair play is, how to play fair, and how to teach children about playing fair;
- early childhood settings to embody policies and actions that include attention to fairness in play at all times.

Vignettes provide examples and these are followed by points of reflection for readers (individually or with others). Practical activities are also suggested for individuals or small groups of colleagues (teachers or students) to tease out some of the complexities associated with the issues raised in the vignettes.

Vignette 6.1: 'all the Lebs [Lebanese] are bad guys'

Abdul aged four, a Lebanese Australian Christian boy living in Bankstown (Sydney), and Brian, aged four, an Anglo-Australian boy living in Cronulla (Sydney) attend the same early childhood centre and have shared a strong friendship for two years. The day after the Cronulla riots (December, 2005), Abdul was very distressed:

Adbul: They said the Lebs are bad guys
Teacher: Who, who said that? [Abdul begins to cry]
Abdul: Brian and the TV. They said all the Lebs are bad guys at the beach and Lebs can't go to the beach.
Teacher: But you're Lebanese and you're not a bad guy.
Abdul: No, Leb.
Teacher: Sorry, you're a Leb and you're not a bad guy and Sarah is a Leb and she's not a bad guy. I know lots of Lebanese people who are not bad guys.
Abdul: But Brian said everyone saw the TV and they all said the Lebs. Brian said I am a Leb bad guy.

(Giugni n.d.: 13)

This distressing conversation between Abdul and the teacher depicts the power of stereotypical 'truths' about an ethnic group of people, in this case Lebanese Australian people. It is seen as a truth because it has been on television and 'everyone saw' it and 'they all' said the Lebs were bad. Young children know that many people watch television and understand the powerful impact that it can have. Brian connected this television story with Abdul and was so influenced by it that he believed the television over his experience of their strong, two-year friendship. As Giugni (n.d.) points out, children's relationships and friendships are complex and can be fragile in similar ways to those of adults. Children are also well informed about racism and how this works in the media.

Reflection point 6.1

- Reflect on the fact that there is no evidence of innocent and naïve children in this conversation.
- Consider the power of Brian's stereotypical representation of Lebanese people.
- Think about the idea that Brian is willing to forego two years of a strong friendship because of what he saw on television one night.
- Add your own points . . .

Practical activities: 'all the Lebs [Lebanese] are bad guys'

- Discuss with colleagues (teachers, students) whether the friendship might be able to survive, and what it might take for this to happen.
- In a small group, make a list of all factors that could be influencing Brian's stance. Use these to sketch ideas about how to approach Abdul, Brian, and the rest of the group of children about this issue.

- List other stereotypes about people of which you are aware and their potential impact.
- In a small group, discuss and list ideas of how teachers might (i) recognize and (ii) teach against stereotypical and racist representations of people as part of their everyday work. Use specific examples (such as Brian and Abdul) to help focus the teaching approaches.
- Add your own points . . .

Vignette 6.2: Mark in the kitchen: Lisa and the Lego™

Mark: The kitchen area featured pink cups and plates, pink aprons, pink shopping baskets, a sink with a pink fascia, tap and cupboard doors, as well as a picture on the wall of a female child engaging in kitchen activities. Despite the pink environment, Mark (3.3) knew a lot about what takes place in a kitchen, which included the preparation of food, the use of kitchen appliances and how to set the table. He played confidently, engaging and directing other children in his kitchen play, and incorporating them into his activity. For example, he warned Bella not to touch the oven because it was hot. Mark was very busy for over 15 minutes, appearing unperturbed when other children entered and left the play of their own accord. He was careful in manipulating china dinnerware, as well as with the placement of china items on the table. He checked twice that the china was in the right place on the table; ensuring items were in line with each chair placed around the table. Mark's play suggested that he was experienced in kitchen play and at incorporating others into it as they came and went. It ended when the teacher called the children over to the mat area. During the 15 minutes, no teachers approached or talked with Mark. It is not known whether the teachers noticed what he was doing.

Lisa: At free playtime, Lisa (4.7) chose to play in the 'Lego™ area' and she was the only girl to do so. Her presence did not draw comment from any of the boys playing near or with her, and she sought their response to her Lego™ creations throughout the time she was there. Lisa created spaceships and rockets, which were similar to many of the items produced by the boys. No teachers came into the Lego™ area during the time Lisa was there. Lisa was the only girl in the classroom not wearing an item of clothing that was pink in colour, and one of the few girls with short hair. She wore a tattoo of a butterfly on her forearm.

- Consider why no teacher approached or talked with Mark during the 15 minutes he was engrossed in play.
- Think about teachers intervening in play and the idea that adults rarely intervene in girls' quiet domestic play even though it is stereotypical and limiting; but they do intervene in boys' superhero play despite high levels of imaginative language and use of symbols (see Wood 2007a).
- Reflect on the idea that the teachers might be avoiding Mark because of the type of play in which he was engaged. Why might they do this?
- If you were the teacher, would you discuss this play with Mark's parents? Why? Why not?
- If you were the teacher, would you discuss this play with Lisa's parents? Why? Why not?
- Add your own points . . .

Vignette 6.3: play and 'recovery'

If play is not always natural, inclusive, or fair, then 'recovery' counts. Julie's (5.0) 'recovery' in play is an important component of her experience in the classroom. She was observed on several occasions to be in 'recovery' from a number of play scenarios where others had positioned her consistently on the periphery. Her personal items (clothes, shoes, backpack, lunch box and food items) suggest that Julie does not have access to as much cultural capital as others in the class do. As one of six girls in the classroom, she is the only one who doesn't wear an item of pink clothing, and the only girl who does not have long hair or wear a decorative item in her hair. The girls spent much time drawing and colouring people wearing pink and floral dresses with handbags, love hearts, flowers and rainbows.

Julie tried on many occasions to enter different play scenarios, and was often allowed to sit near the play, but was excluded from participating fully through a lack of sharing of resources and positioning of bodies to deny entry to the physical play space. When leaving of her own accord to begin play by herself, groups of boys on the move around the room often overtook Julie. In 'recovery' mode, Julie responds to the actions of others by rolling her eyes and shaking her head a number of times at the other children before moving away to another space/activity. When leaving the play, at no time did she look back at the other children, teacher or the researcher to ascertain if anyone had noticed how the play was unfolding, or her reaction to it.

Moving away from the play, eye rolling and head shaking is a form of recovery that seems powerful and dignified for Julie. It allows her to adopt a position where she passes judgment on others, and where her judgments separate her from the biased and unfair actions of others. In these moments of recovery, perhaps she is more powerful because she has distanced herself from the other children in the room – not needing to, nor wanting to belong to a group whose actions and intentions she deems objectionable. For Julie, 'recovery' seems as crucial as the play itself, because of the way others position her. Her recovery strategy enables her to reposition herself without the aid or intervention of an adult, and seemingly without the knowledge of an adult. A strategy to separate oneself physically and ideologically from others is isolating but it preserves self-respect and allows Julie, throughout the day, to maintain face in an environment in which she is often excluded because of the unjust judgments and actions of others.

Reflection point 6.3

- Think about Julie's situation and the possibility that she removed herself from the play as respite from the unfair situations she experienced.
- What are the implications for Julie's sense of belonging?
- Do you see Julie's actions as legitimate in the circumstances? Why? Why not?
- What could staff do to support Julie and others like her?
- The teachers may not know what is happening or the sophistication of how the girls are working in concert to marginalize Julie. The girls are not reprimanded, which condones their actions and makes it more likely that it will continue. How can this cycle be interrupted?
- Add your own points . . .

Practical activities: play and 'recovery'

- With a partner or small group, think about children with whom you have worked. Recall and discuss examples of behaviour that might be similar to what Julie has experienced; and the recovery action that she took.
- Discuss with others how you might identify children such as Julie.
- Plan with a partner or small group of colleagues (students, teachers) the action you might take to support children in situations similar to Julie. Think about Julie, the other children who are excluding her, as well as the rest of the group.

- Discuss what might be included in centre policies, action plans and professional learning for staff to prevent unjust play like this occurring.
- Add your own points . . .

Vignette 6.4: using physical force to take toys

Rachel (3.7) and Michael (3.6) were sitting next to each other at a table doing puzzles. David (3.5) was close by, playing with a dinosaur, also at the table. David was the shortest and smallest child in the class. He had a 'rat's tail' in his hair (a strip of hair at the centre back of his head that was noticeably longer than the rest of his hair). His ethnicity is unknown but his physical features and skin colour indicate that he is not an Anglo-Australian child and is possibly of mixed heritage.

Rachel finished the puzzle and began watching David playing with the dinosaur. She leaned toward him and used physical force to overpower him and take the dinosaur from him. There was no exchange of words but both children looked at the researcher who was holding the video camera, perhaps expecting the adult to stop Rachel taking the dinosaur from David, but this did not occur. David made strong eye contact with the researcher, perhaps appealing for assistance in this nonverbal and partially concealed way. If it had worked, it would have meant that David was not subjected to the indignity of having to seek help from the teacher publicly, thus saving face. When she had the dinosaur in her hands, Rachel stood for a while holding it. She did not play with it, which suggests that she simply did not want David to have it and exerted her physical power and dominance to take it from him.

David returned a short time later with another dinosaur, stood behind the table at a 'safe' distance and began playing with it, only to be set upon suddenly from behind by a boy (Jeremy) who was considerably taller than he was. Rachel responded immediately and moved from her sitting position at the table to David. In the meantime, Jeremy had wrapped his arms around David, engulfing the arm that held the dinosaur and overpowering him, and dragged him away. Rachel assisted, pushing from the front and ensuring that David was manoeuvred behind a screen where Jeremy took the dinosaur from David's hand. A short time later, when Rachel was busy helping Michael with a puzzle, David returned with the dinosaur that Rachel had taken from him. This time Michael became interested in the dinosaur and he attempted to remove it physically from David's grasp. But Michael was further away from David, and this time David seemed to be ready. He quickly moved the dinosaur out of Michael's reach and managed to keep hold of it. Michael returned his attention to the puzzle.

In the space of about 5 minutes, both Rachel and Jeremy physically manipulated David in their efforts to remove the dinosaurs from his hands. David was overpowered both times but was able to thwart the third attempt. After events such as these, David played by himself for long periods. No teachers saw what happened and the way the series of events 'played' out suggested that it was not the first time that it had occurred. David's small physical stature and nonmembership of the dominant Anglo-Australian group appear to be significant factors in how he was treated. The quick, quiet and subtle removal of toys by stealth and the physical manipulation of David's body attracted little, if any attention from other children. Play events where physical size has been used to intimidate others and prevent them from playing have been documented by Danby and Baker (1998); and size, skin colour and proficiency with English were factors in how two Anglo-Australian boys who were much younger than Mick managed to marginalize him and prevent him from playing (Campbell 2005).

Reflection point 6.4

- Consider that David might have been subjected to this type of physical force on occasions other than those discussed here. Why might this have happened?
- How might this affect David's sense of belonging to the group?
- Reflect on how this could have happened without staff taking any action.
- Being able to overpower David without any reproach from teachers increases the likelihood that it will occur again.
- What action do you think should be taken in this situation and others like it?
- Add your own points . . .

Practical activities: using physical force to take toys

- With a partner or small group, discuss how to prevent this type of thing happening in your work situation. Make a list of things you could do to prevent it from occurring. Saying nothing condones actions such as these.
- Observe carefully and listen for situations where children may be overpowered (like David). Be aware of eye contact as a way of appealing for assistance that is less likely to alert perpetrators and therefore cause less 'trouble' for the victim. Be alert to factors that may be involved: size, skin colour, member of nondominant group, language proficiency.

- Discuss actions you could take with individual children (the 'victim' and the perpetrators) and with the whole group as ways to prevent unfair practices such as these occurring.
- Discuss how teaching about injustice and unfairness can be part of everyday classroom life.
- Add your own points . . .

Vignette 6.5: competent children?

In the hubbub of everyday classroom life, sometimes children are overlooked unintentionally, sometimes because teachers are busy, and sometimes teachers ignore particular behaviour in an attempt to reduce or eliminate its frequency. On other occasions, it can be difficult for teachers to identify the significance of particular events because of their subtlety. The following seems to be one such occasion.

When the teacher left the room for morning tea, Sarah (2.9) put her thumb in her mouth, moved to the corner cushion area with a soft toy and lay down. About ten minutes later, she stood up and moved to the main area of the room where she began to access the dress-up play space. Sarah's response to the teacher leaving the room indicated a high level of competence (resilience even?) in terms of regulating an emotional response to an event in one's environment. She demonstrated the capacity to self-manage the intensity of her response and accessed objects and spaces that gave both acknowledgement and support for her emotional needs at that time (e.g., an object held close to her body, and an environment that was comfortable and removed from the main area and in which she could position her body in a particular way). Sarah also demonstrated the capability to 'recover' from the event and return to play activities in the room.

What is perplexing about this scenario is that Sarah's response and movements did not draw attention from any of the three teachers in the room. This may be because they position Sarah as 'competent and capable' (previous observations and interactions with teachers and other children suggest this) and therefore able to manage her feelings herself. Perhaps Sarah wasn't 'seen' at all, because the intensity of her response didn't draw or warrant the attention of adults in the room. That is, she didn't cry, fuss, or seek out another adult for support. Whatever it was, staff could have acknowledged Sarah's vulnerability at this point in her day. It need not draw attention to her emotional state – it could be subtle, such as being close to her or placing a hand on hers.

Reflection point 6.5

- Our views about children and childhood ensure that we see the 'world' from particular perspectives. The teachers see Sarah (2.9) as competent and capable. Reflect critically on the idea that the competent and capable discourse could be working to dehumanize some children's experiences because they are seen to be coping in the moment.
- What would you have done if you had noticed Sarah? Why?
- How might this experience have affected Sarah's sense of belonging?
- Add your own points . . .

Practical activities: competent children?

- With others, discuss your response to the idea that the competent and capable discourse could be working to dehumanize some children's experiences because they are seen to be coping.
- Brainstorm with others how you might be able to use this information in your daily work with young children, giving specific examples.
- Add your own points . . .

Vignette 6.6: physical size in play

Physical size can give children access to particular roles and identities in play, simultaneously creating opportunities and vulnerabilities. Children who are taller and heavier can use their size to control space, objects and people. Children who are smaller in both height and weight can use their size to create a perception of vulnerability and as a way of appealing for empathy about a perceived lack of fairness. *Groups* of smaller children sometimes work together to exercise power over larger children to regain space and control in play. Size can denote the gain or loss of an identity in play if a costume doesn't fit or someone's size doesn't 'match' their preferred role. Size is about actual physicality but also about presence by perception. It is about how children occupy a space in a physical sense, but also how they move through space using their size as a tool for exercising different types of power, and how other children and teachers respond to both. In play, size is relational – it is about how small or large one is in relation to others, objects and environments, and what this means in terms of the roles and identities one adopts in play, and the arguments one can employ to justify position(s).

Reflection point 6.6

- Think about children you have worked with who are taller and heavier and use their size to control space, objects and people. What are the consequences of this happening? Who benefits? Who doesn't? What can teachers do?
- Think about children you have worked with who are smaller in both height and weight and use their size to create a perception of vulnerability as a way of appealing for empathy about a perceived lack of fairness. What are the consequences of this for the child, the staff and the other children?
- Consider the possible actions staff could take if a child's size doesn't match their preferred role in play.
- Add your own points . . .

Practical activities: physical size in play

- With a partner or small group, discuss your experiences of groups of smaller children working together to exercise power over larger children to regain space and control in play.
- Explore strategies for identifying how and where this occurs.
- Discuss whether staff should take any action in such situations and list advantages and disadvantages of doing so.
- Add your own points . . .

Vignette 6.7: who gets what roles?

In a play scenario about teenagers involving six boys, Max (5.3), the tallest boy, used his height, age and ethnicity (Anglo-Australian) to commandeer particular dress-up clothes (a jacket and a hat) and claim the central role. Other children had to negotiate for roles and clothes, and one ended up as Max's pet. There were power plays about clothes and accessories; about who got what and why; who 'likes' whom in the play; who can't die in the play, and who has access to particular spaces. The way the roles were decided showed that not all children were able to participate equally in the decision-making process. Alongside height, age and ethnicity, knowledge of teenagers, teenage clothing and popular culture associated with teenagers were highly valued. The play took over the 'home' area and became the teenagers' bedroom and the pet's bed. As the play progressed, roles were elevated from 'teenager' to 'teenager dad', 'teenager brother' and 'teenager family', with a similar hierarchy evident in decisions about the roles and who would play them. There was a significant interruption when the teacher called Max away from the play to complete a painting and required him to remove his teenager clothes. His role in, and control of, the play were at risk. Max asked if the 'pet' could do the painting with him but the teacher was not sympathetic to his request. When pressured by the teacher to start the painting, Max asked another boy to hold the clothes while the painting was completed. The 'pet' heard this conversation and went to Max, who handed over the jacket and hat saying '. . . look after this for me.' The 'pet' was trusted to keep the clothes safe for Max and put the jacket and hat in the crook of his arm.

Reflection point 6.7

- Decisions about roles occur when play begins and are key points for observing relationships of power at work. Recall some play scenarios from your work, or observe some. Think about factors that are often involved: ethnicity, skin colour, gender, height, size, proficiency with English, cultural capital (e.g., personal items such as clothing, shoes, bag, and so on), knowledge of popular culture; and how these factors affect decisions about the roles children have in the play and who makes the decisions.
- What do you consider to be fair and unfair? Why?
- What action could you take on the basis of what you consider to be fair and unfair?
- Talk with others about your reflection and seek their views. Discuss similarities and differences in views and the reasons for them.
- Add your own points . . .

Conclusion

Much free play in early childhood settings reproduces relations of power in society. Thus those who are already in powerful positions can be further enabled and those who are already marginalized can be further compromised in play. Children can use power in overt and covert ways, acting quickly and silently, and attempting to avoid detection (as can be seen in the way David was physically manipulated); or being overt, as Brian was in his statements about the 'Lebs'. Learning about how play can be unjust and inequitable provides opportunities for thinking about how marginalization occurs. Understanding how marginalization occurs can facilitate ways of addressing unfairness in play, and ways of teaching children about 'playing fair'. It also sets up opportunities for finding ways of teaching children to build relationships in different and more equitable ways. For teachers it involves learning about who you are and how you came to have the understandings you have about yourself and others. As well as taking actions such as these, early childhood centres require policies that emphasize socially just and equitable curricula, learning, pedagogies and assessment practices.

Suggested readings

Danby, S. and Baker, C. (1998) How to be masculine in the block area, *Childhood*, 5(12): 151–75.

Mundine, K. and Giugni, M. (2006) *Diversity and Difference: Lighting the Spirit of Identity*. Canberra: Early Childhood Australia.

7 Play and early childhood curriculum documents

This chapter investigates the way in which play is conceptualized in early childhood curriculum documents from Hong Kong, Australia, Sweden, and England. We review these curriculum guidelines for before-school settings for the place accorded to play, the connections between play and learning, and the ways in which play is to be enacted in the curriculum. Part of this review includes the constructions of play articulated in these curriculum documents and those discussed in this book (play as learning, fun, hard work, natural, serious business, fair, and rules for play). The goals for this chapter are:

- to investigate how play is conceptualized and encouraged in a range of curriculum documents written for children attending before-school settings;
- to explore connections between these curriculum documents and the constructions of play in this book.

Play, recent research and early childhood curriculum documents

In the Western world, the early years have been the focus of much recent government attention. One of the reasons for this attention has been the results of cost benefit analyses applied to early childhood programmes, which have shown that investment in the early years is a cost saving device for the future. It produces higher tax revenues through better jobs and reduces future costs to society because of lower criminal justice system expenditure and fewer welfare payments (see Belfield et al. 2006). An outcome of cost-benefit analyses has been the proliferation of not only research in the early years but of curriculum guides for the years prior to compulsory schooling.

Play is given a significant place in recent policy and curriculum documents, and play-based approaches are the way in which educational outcomes are to be achieved (Wood 2009). In addition to outcomes, the preference for educational versions of play in recent curriculum documents has been accompanied by a focus on learning (not just development), the changed role of teachers and the inclusion of 'content'. In contrast, widely accepted views of (free) play are that it is freely chosen, personally driven and intrinsically motivated. The way in which play is conceptualized in recent policy and curriculum documents challenges notions of free play and has produced concerns about whether play can and should be used to achieve specific educational (instrumental?) purposes. That is, given that play is the crux of child-centred pedagogy, should it be used to achieve learning outcomes that are derived from what Wood (2007a: 310) has called 'regulated curriculum and assessment frameworks'. The curriculum documents from England for children from birth to the age of 5 years are highly regulated (by legislation) and teachers are required to complete an assessment profile for each child at the end of this stage of learning.

The educational emphasis on play in recent policy and curriculum documents has come about at the same time that research has challenged traditional notions of play – in particular what has been called 'free' or 'discovery' play (e.g., Sylva et al. 2004; Ryan 2005; Wood 2007a). For instance, Ryan (2005) has shown how play in child-centred approaches is political and how power relationships operate under the guise of freedom to choose. Other unease about curriculum documents that include 'educational' play has occurred over questions raised about 'whose purposes and intentions are paramount . . .' and what are 'the modes, intentions and outcomes of adult intervention' (Wood 2009: 166–7). These concerns sit alongside the long-held worry by the US National Association for the Education of Young Children (NAEYC) about the threat to play posed by the push for academic curricula and teaching methods for young children (Bredekamp 1987; Bredekamp and Copple 1997; Copple and Bredekamp 2009).

The curriculum documents selected for review are recent publications. The Hong Kong preprimary curriculum was published in 2006. The documents from Australia and England were published in 2009 and 2008 respectively. The Swedish curriculum is currently being rewritten, after being published first in 1998 and revised in 2006. We begin the review with the preprimary curriculum from Hong Kong, the current version of which was published in 2006. Its antecedents in 1996 and 1984 encapsulated several of the basic principles of the 2006 document (Fung and Lee 2008). Each section begins with contextual information about the respective curriculum document for each country.

Hong Kong

The *Guide to the Pre-primary Curriculum* (hereafter the Guide) (The Curriculum Development Council [CDC] 2006) was written for preprimary contexts in Hong Kong that serve children aged 2 to 6 years. Features of the Guide include:

- it is a revision of the 1996 Guide (CDC 1996);
- it is just over 100 pages in length;
- it includes sections about curriculum planning, learning and teaching, assessment, transition to primary schooling, and home-school relationships;
- it includes eight appendices that identify a range of complementary information such as developmental characteristics of children from birth to the age of six, values and attitudes for incorporation into the curriculum, and children's behaviours that are concerning.

Settings catering for children in the preprimary years are encouraged to adopt the recommendations of the Guide. In line with other educational reforms in Hong Kong, the Guide emphasizes the development of the whole person and life-long learning.

Despite recent efforts to the contrary, the school-leaving examination dominates education in Hong Kong and has a pervasive influence not only on secondary and primary schooling but also on kindergarten education (Chan and Chan 2003). Accordingly, kindergartens experience substantial pressure to 'adopt formal academic curriculum as well as test-oriented and teacher centred approaches' (Chan and Chan 2003: 11). Academic and test oriented approaches are considered necessary to prepare children to compete for admission to primary schools that have academically oriented and difficult curriculum, and which are favoured by parents (Chan and Chan 2003: 11). Consequently, parents prefer their children to attend a kindergarten that provides a significant amount of instruction in reading, writing and counting, so that they can be admitted to a good primary school and develop a strong foundation for future success (Wong 2006). This is despite the 1996 and 2006 versions of the *Guide to the Pre-primary Curriculum* recommending a child-centred approach, focusing on the all-round development of children, and identifying the importance of 'play, learning and care' as the 'three essential elements of daily activities in a pre-primary institution' (CDC 1996: 63). Confucian heritage maintains a strong influence in Hong Kong society. It includes the importance of being polite, righteous, honest, valuing hard work in order to establish a good foundation for becoming successful members of society; and the belief that success is based on persistence and effort (Wong 2006).

Most kindergartens in Hong Kong teach reading, writing and number work (some as early as three years), use workbooks, set homework regularly, and use tests and examinations (Opper 1992). More recently, both Lau (2006) and Wong (2006) have indicated that the formal and academic nature of kindergartens in Hong Kong has prevailed. Such activities are likely to be seen as inappropriate for children in kindergartens in many Western societies (see for example, Bredekamp and Copple 1997; Copple and Bredekamp 2009). Wong (2006) has also suggested that many parents hold the belief that superior kindergartens provide much instruction on writing and counting, and inferior kindergartens engage children in very few of these tasks. A child-centred or progressive approach sits in contrast to some of the more traditional curriculums and pedagogy found in kindergartens in Hong Kong, and some of the ideas expressed about what parents want kindergartens to provide. Child-centred approaches also create conflict for kindergarten teachers in Hong Kong (Li 2004) and teachers can experience many challenges if they try to enact the concept of 'learning through play' in their kindergartens (Cheng 2001).

The Guide advocates assessment approaches that create a comprehensive picture of children's performance and overall development, and it acknowledges the limitations of examinations. The purpose of assessment is to focus on 'measuring children's development and learning' (CDC 2006: 61). At the completion of the preprimary stage, children's 'developmental abilities and performance are examined' (CDC 2006: 61). This occurs in the four areas of development (physical, cognitive and language, affective and social, aesthetic development) and in the six learning areas (physical fitness and health; language; early mathematics; science and technology; self and society, and arts). Indicators are provided for the developmental areas in the Guide and teachers are also referred to a document that lists performance indicators for preprimary institutions.

Table 7.1 shows connections between keys ideas in this book and the content of the Hong Kong *Guide to the Pre-primary Curriculum*. Preprimary institutions are encouraged to 'Adopt play as a learning strategy' (CDC 2006: 41) and accordingly, play has a significant role in the philosophy of the Guide. It states that learning occurs through play (p. 12) and that play activities should be happy (p. 12), 'inspiring and fun' (p. 13). In contrast to some of the developmentally appropriate type of play that is encouraged by Bredekamp and Copple (1997) and Copple and Bredekamp (2009), the Guide states that at the age of 5–6 years, children should be 'Able to play competitive games like chess' (p. 92). The Guide suggests that playing appropriately is as an indicator of 'normal' development. What causes concern is therefore revealed by play that does not conform to the norm, or goes beyond the boundaries of what is seen as acceptable forms of play. To guide practitioners with the task of identifying what is normal, examples are provided (see the point 'Not natural' in Table 7.1 for illustrations of what is not 'natural' or normal at certain ages). Fair

Table 7.1 Play and the Hong Kong *Guide to the Pre-primary Curriculum* (CDC 2006)

Understandings of play	Links to the Hong Kong Guide to the Pre-primary Curriculum
Play as learning (see Chapter 1)	'How do children learn . . . through play?' (p. 12) 'Through play, they can learn in a self-motivated, committed, pleasurable, relaxing and effective manner' (p. 12) '. . . play is an indispensable and important tool for facilitating children's learning' (p. 51)
Play as fun; play as hard work (see Chapter 2): '. . . play is equated with fun . . . fun is contingent on who, when and where.'	'Children's abilities should be developed through play activities that are inspiring and fun' (p. 13) 'Children are fond of play, which enables them to enjoy the freedom and fun of sharing and working with others' (p. 41)
Naturally produced play (play is children's natural way of learning) (see Chapter 3)	'Play is a happy learning experience' (p. 12) 'Play is fun by nature' (p. 53) At 5–6 years, 'Able to play competitive games like chess' (p. 92) *Not natural* at 2 years: 'Does not show any pretend play' (p. 100); at 3 years: 'Does not participate in pretend play' (p. 100); at 4 years: 'Ignores other children and prefers playing on his [sic] own' (p. 100)
Play as serious business (. . . turning the documentation of play into a serious business) (see Chapter 4)	'Every child should have a chance to exhibit his/her work' (p. 48)
Rules of/for play (see Chapter 5)	At 4–5 years, 'Willing to observe rules of the games when playing with other children' (p. 90)
Playing fair (see Chapter 6)	'For older children, physical play in groups can further cultivate team spirit and help them learn the principle of fair play' (p. 23) 'Fair play' is an attitude to be incorporated into the curriculum (p. 94) By 5–6 years, children are able to 'understand the principle of fair play . . .' (p. 92)

play is mentioned several times and is encouraged, as is developing a sense of team spirit as an attitude to be incorporated into the curriculum. By the age of 4–5 years, children should not only know the rules of games but be willing to observe them; and by the age of 5–6 years, they should be able to understand the principle of team spirit (p. 92).

Play is described as an 'indispensable part of children's growth' (p. 53) and teachers are instructed to 'make good use of play as a major element for constructing curriculum' (p. 53). Three pages of the Guide are devoted to explaining 'Approaches to Learning and Teaching', which are to occur through play. Links are made to traditional areas of child development, with the Guide (CDC 2006: 51) stating that, through play, children 'can develop their physical, intellectual, social, creative and thinking abilities'. Key elements for play are identified as toys, playmates, the environment, and allocation of an appropriate amount of time for play to occur. Five roles for teachers during play are identified (provider, observer, participant, intervener, inspirer). The three traditional noninterventionist roles for teachers of provider, observer and participant (see Bennett et al. 1997) have been extended to include intervener and inspirer. In terms of intervention in children's play, teachers are advised to consider children's abilities and the level of difficulty of the task. If necessary, they may 'intervene in an indirect and interesting way, and finish the game without spoiling children's confidence and interest' (p. 53). Teachers are encouraged to inspire play that stimulates thinking, creativity and imagination.

Despite the significance given to play-based learning in the 2006 Guide and its predecessors, Confucian values find their way into the curriculum and many are endorsed in the 'Proposed set of values and attitudes for incorporation into the school curriculum' (CDC 2006: 94). In addition, research has shown that the longstanding parental preference for academic curricula is proving hard to shift. For instance, Li's (2003; 28) study concluded that learning in kindergartens 'would be conducted in a teacher-directed mode', perhaps because teachers encounter many challenges if they try to enact the concept of learning through play (e.g., Cheng 2001; Li 2003, 2004). Fung and Lee (2008) make a fundamental point in questioning whether preschool teachers in Hong Kong have beliefs and practices that are compatible with the child-centred approaches reflected in the Guide. There is also concern that the increasing accountability and quality assurance measures in Hong Kong could cause teachers to resist or creatively 'adapt' the child-centred play based approaches encouraged in the Guide (Fung and Lee 2008).

Reflection point 7.1

Discuss with others, reflecting on the following ideas:

- Children should be able to play competitive games like chess by the age of 5–6 years.
- Parental preferences for academic curricula prevail over play-based approaches.

> • Why might Western ideas such as play be included in curriculum when cultural values are different.

Australia

Belonging, Being and Becoming: The Early Years Learning Framework for Australia (hereafter the Framework) (Commonwealth of Australia 2009) was published in July 2009 and is the first national approach for early childhood educators in that country. As part of a national strategy for early childhood education, the Framework is to be used by early childhood practitioners in their daily work with children from birth to the age of five years. It is 47 pages in length, including a glossary and bibliography. A vision of children deserving the best start in life is found in the introduction, as is the influence of human capital theory: 'All children have the best start in life to create a better future for themselves and for the nation' (p. 5). The introduction also acknowledges the emphasis on play-based learning and that the Framework is guided by United Nations principles on the Rights of the Child (the Convention). In this regard specific recognition is given to 'children's right to play' (p. 5). Another feature of note in the introduction is the social justice commitment to 'closing the gap in educational achievement between Indigenous and non-Indigenous Australians within a decade' (p. 6). To this end a document providing guidance about 'ensuring cultural security' (p. 6) for Aboriginal and Torres Strait Islander children and their families is to be developed.

The Framework is characterized by its emphasis on play-based learning, its focus on learning and development, intentional teaching, and the active promotion of learning outcomes. As well as the introduction, the Framework has five other main sections:

- a vision for children's learning;
- early childhood pedagogy;
- principles;
- practice;
- learning outcomes for children birth to 5 years.

The vision for children's learning is encapsulated in a diagram that shows children's learning as the focal point of the vision; it is surrounded by the interrelated elements of Principles, Learning Outcomes and Practice, which are framed by the concepts Belonging, Being and Becoming. The section about Practice names eight ways in which pedagogical practice promotes children's learning, one of which is Learning through Play. The final section about

Learning Outcomes is by far the largest part, occupying over half of the document with 26 of the 47 pages devoted to examples showing how the outcomes for children are evident; and examples of how educators can promote learning associated with each outcome. The five outcomes are:

- children have a strong sense of identity;
- children are connected with and contribute to their world;
- children have a strong sense of wellbeing;
- children are confident and involved learners;
- children are effective communicators.

Play is mentioned several times in the discussion of each outcome. The length of the section about outcomes attests to the significance attached to it. The importance is further emphasized by statements such as 'Educators plan with each child and the outcomes in mind' (p. 19).

The Framework signifies the importance of assessment for learning and provides guidance about how assessment works with the principles, practice, pedagogy and outcomes. One purpose of assessment for learning is to 'determine the extent to which all children are progressing toward realising learning outcomes, and if not, what might be impeding their progress' (Commonwealth of Australia 2009: 17). The five outcomes statements are described as 'key reference points against which children's progress can be identified, documented and communicated to families, other early childhood professionals and educators in schools' (Commonwealth of Australia 2009: 17). Examples of behaviours that show children are demonstrating the outcomes are provided, as are the sorts of things practitioners can do to promote the learning associated with particular outcomes.

Table 7.2 shows connections between keys ideas in this book about play and the content of *Belonging, Being and Becoming: The Early Years Learning Framework for Australia* (Commonwealth of Australia 2009). With its specific emphasis on play, the Framework describes play-based learning as 'a context for learning through which children organise and make sense of their social worlds, as they engage actively with people, objects and representations' (Commonwealth of Australia 2009: 6). Specific connections are made between play and learning that relate to expanding children's thinking and their desire to know and learn. There are almost no direct references to play as fun or play as hard work: the closest to fun is that children show enthusiasm for participating in physical play. Drawing on the concepts of naturally produced play (see Chapter 3 in this book) the point is made in the Framework that immersion in play provides enjoyment in 'being'. But 'naturally' produced dramatic play can also enable the exploration of different perspectives and identities; and with reflection and investigation, can lead to the solution of problems. Children are expected to participate in decision making

Table 7.2 Play and *Belonging, Being and Becoming: The Early Years Learning Framework for Australia* (The Commonwealth of Australia 2009)

Understandings of play	Links to Belonging, Being and Becoming: The Early Years Learning Framework for Australia
Play as learning (see Chapter 1)	'. . . a specific emphasis on play-based learning' (p. 5) 'Play can expand children's thinking and enhance their desire to know and learn' (p. 15) 'Play is a context for learning . . .' (p. 9)
Play as fun; play as hard work (see Chapter 2): '. . . play is equated with fun . . . fun is contingent on who, when and where.'	'Show enthusiasm for participating in physical play . . .' (p. 32)
Naturally produced play (play is children's natural way of learning) (see Chapter 3)	'Children's immersion in their play illustrates how play enables them to simply enjoy being' (p. 15) 'Explore different identities and points of view in dramatic play' (p. 23) 'Use the processes of play, reflection and investigation to solve problems' (p. 36)
Play as serious business (. . . turning the documentation of play into a serious business) (see Chapter 4)	'Key components of learning in each outcome are expanded to provide examples of evidence that educators may observe in children as they learn [play]' (p. 19)
Rules of/for play (see Chapter 5)	. . . 'plan opportunities for children to participate in meaningful ways in group discussions and shared decision-making about rules and expectations' (p. 26)
Playing fair (see Chapter 6)	. . . Early childhood practitioners 'actively support the inclusion of all children in play, help children to recognize when play is unfair and offer constructive ways to build a caring, fair and inclusive learning community' (p. 15)

about rules. The Framework has a strong emphasis on playing fair and identifies the role of practitioners in creating and maintaining a 'caring, fair and inclusive learning community' (p. 15). It also states that practitioners should assist children to know when play is unfair, and why it is unfair, and to offer alternatives.

The challenge for practitioners is to create a play-based approach that uses outcomes to plan for each child but that also takes account of children's strengths and interests. Using outcomes to plan play-based curricula is quite different from the emergent approaches that typify many early childhood curricula. Reflection point 2 asks readers to think about some of the implications of a learning framework that is play-based and values intentional teaching, but which also requires practitioners to plan according to learning outcomes.

Reflection point 7.2

Discuss the following ideas with others and reflect on them.

- List the advantages and disadvantages of using learning outcomes to guide planning for children's learning.
- Are play-based curricula contradictory to using learning outcomes for planning curricula? Why? Why not?
- Why is there an emphasis on intentional teaching?
- Why do you think there is a focus on children's learning?
- Why might the document have such a big emphasis on learning outcomes?
- If 'free' play means that play is freely chosen, personally driven and intrinsically motivated, then what is compromised when play-based approaches use outcomes?

The Framework acknowledges the importance of play-based learning, values intentional teaching and links outcomes directly with play-based learning. It aligns with recent research that has contested traditional notions of play; in particular what has been called 'free' or 'discovery' play and the lack of intervention by teachers in this play. The Framework (Commonwealth of Australia 2009: 15) has responded with the concept of intentional teaching, where educators are 'deliberate, purposeful and thoughtful in their decisions and action.' The question is whether play should be used in an instrumental way to achieve learning outcomes that are derived from what Wood (2007a: 310) called 'regulated curriculum and assessment frameworks'. We take this up in the last section of this chapter.

Sweden

In Sweden children start compulsory schooling at the age of seven and nearly all children aged six (98 per cent) attend the noncompulsory preschool class, which is mostly a half-day provision (minimum 525 hours) and is free (Gunnarsson 2007a). The national curriculum for compulsory schooling (Lpo 94) has been altered to include this preschool class with the idea of easing the transition from the preschool class to the curriculum of compulsory schooling. From the beginning of 2003, universal preschool was introduced for all children aged 4–5 years for a minimum of 525 hours per year. The Swedish education system has an integrated approach to curriculum that spans the ages of 1–20 years and incorporates three curricula. *Lpfö 98* (Swedish Ministry of Education and Science 2006) is the curriculum for children aged 1–5 years. The curriculum for grades 1–9 includes the preschool class for children aged 6 years; and a curriculum for upper secondary school (grades 10–12) completes the integrated approach. The integrated approach is evident in the connections among each and the three curricula 'are linked by a shared view on knowledge, development and learning, and cover the first 20 years of the life-long learning philosophy of Swedish society' (Gunnarsson 2007a: 1244).

Curriculum for the Pre-school Lpfö 98 (Swedish Ministry of Education and Science 2006) is the first of the three integrated curricula and is designed for children aged 1–5 years. It is 14 pages in length and has two major sections:

* fundamental values and tasks of the preschool;
* goals and guidelines.

The curriculum was written for the purposes of continuity and cohesion in preschool curriculum and pedagogy. *Lpfö 98* makes strong statements about the democratic principles on which Swedish preschools are established and explains that they are charged with assisting children to acquire the democratic values on which Swedish society is based. Preschool centres develop their own curricula and pedagogical methods from the values and principles outlined in *Lpfö 98* (OECD, 2006). Because *Lpfö 98* is comparatively brief and identifies fundamental values, goals and guidelines, decisions about how the goals are achieved and the curriculum is enacted are left to the teachers.

The first major section, 'Fundamental values and tasks of the preschool', begins with a strong statement about democracy: 'Democracy forms the foundation of the pre-school' (Swedish Ministry of Education and Science 2006: 3). Other fundamental values that are promoted in preschools include 'the inviolability of human life, individual freedom and integrity, the equal value of all people, equality between the genders as well as solidarity with the weak and vulnerable' (Swedish Ministry of Education and Science 2006: 3). These values are considered the ethical responsibility of preschool teachers to enact as part of the preschool curriculum. Learning about respect, care and consideration of others, justice for all and the rights of all are therefore essential aspects of preschool activity (Swedish Ministry of Education and Science 2006). Children are encouraged to form their own opinions and make choices accordingly. They are seen as competent learners and thinkers, actively involved in all aspects of preschool life, and as learning from peers as well as adults. Pedagogical activities are oriented to the needs of all children and children's differing background experiences are to be respected and valued. Preschools present opportunities for children to learn about the cultural diversity of the Swedish population as well as environmental issues and conservation. Consequently, preschools are important in laying the foundations for lifelong learning.

In the second section of *Lpfö 98: Goals and guidelines*, there are five subsections:

- norms and values;
- development and learning;
- influence of the child;
- preschool and home;
- cooperation between the preschool class, the school and the leisure-time centre.

The goals in the five subsections provide direction for the work of the preschool and the guidelines identify the responsibilities of all who work in the preschool. Children's development and learning is emphasized; and the pedagogical activities in the programme should 'stimulate and challenge the child's learning and development' (Swedish Ministry of Education and Science 2006: 9).

The team working in the preschool is mentioned specifically as being responsible for ensuring that what occurs in the preschool is aimed at the goals of the curriculum (Swedish Ministry of Education and Science 2006: 8). Play has an important role because it is 'the basis of preschool activity in that it fosters thinking, imagination, creativity, language, and cooperation' (Gunnarson 2007a: 1244). One could contend that this interpretation by Gunnarson seems somewhat utilitarian, but no more so (perhaps less) than the way play is conceptualized in any of the other curriculum documents considered here. While goals are identified and it is left to the teachers to make curricula decisions about how to enact them, the goals 'describe processes rather than final outcomes' and they are '*goals to strive for*, rather than *goals to be attained*' (Gunnarson 2007b: 1259; emphasis in original). Therefore there is no expectation that the goals will be 'explicitly achieved in terms of individual development and learning of the child' (Gunnarson 2007a: 1245). Similarly, individual child outcomes are not 'formally assessed in terms of grades and evaluations, since children might attend preschool at different ages and over varying periods of time' (Gunnarson 2007a: 1245). The brevity of the document; its philosophical orientation as opposed to detailed directives; the notion of striving for goals rather than expecting them to be achieved explicitly for individual children, and the lack of formal assessment in terms of grades and evaluations, set this curriculum document apart from many others.

Table 7.3 (Swedish Ministry of Education and Science 2006) shows how play is conceptualized in the Swedish preschool curriculum document in relation to the ideas about play in this book. The strong alignment with play and its association with development and learning is evident throughout the document, but the magnitude of play in and of itself is signalled by the

Table 7.3 Play and *Curriculum for the Pre-school Lpfö 98*

Understandings of play	Links to Curriculum for the Pre-school Lpfö 98
Play as learning (see Chapter 1)	'Conscious use of play to promote the development and learning of each child should be an omnipresent activity in the preschool' (p. 6)
Play as fun; play as hard work (see Chapter 2): '. . . play is equated with fun . . . the notion of fun is contingent on who, when and where.'	'. . . develop their curiosity and enjoyment at the same time as the ability to play and learn' (p. 9) 'Activities should promote play, creativity and enjoyment of learning as well as focus on and strengthen the child's interest in learning and mastering new experiences, knowledge and skills' (p. 9)
Naturally produced play (play is children's natural way of learning) (see Chapter 3)	'Play and enjoyment in learning in all its various forms stimulates the imagination, insight, communication and the ability to think symbolically as well as the ability to cooperate and solve problems' (p. 6)
Play as serious business (. . . turning the documentation of play into a serious business) (see Chapter 4)	
Rules of/for play (see Chapter 5)	'Democracy forms the foundation of the pre-school' (p. 3) Fundamental values promoted in preschools include 'the inviolability of human life, individual freedom and integrity, the equal value of all people, equality between the genders as well as solidarity with the weak and vulnerable' (p. 3)
Playing fair (see Chapter 6)	'Care and consideration towards other persons, as well as justice and equality, in addition to the rights of each individual shall be emphasized and made explicit in all pre-school activity' (p. 3) 'The pre-school should work to counteract traditional gender patterns and gender roles' (p. 4) 'The pre-school can help to ensure that children from national minorities, and children with a foreign background receive support in developing a multicultural belonging' (p. 5)

statement that it should be 'an omnipresent activity in the preschool' (p. 6). Play is connected with curiosity and enjoyment of learning, and as a way to develop creative abilities and express them. As the document is framed by democratic principles, justice, equality and the rights of all individuals are expected to be part of the ethos of Swedish preschools. Preschools are also expected to play a part in enculturing migrants and refugees into Swedish society.

Reflection point 7.3 encourages readers to think about some of the underlying elements of the Swedish preschool curriculum.

Reflection point 7.3

Discuss the following ideas with others, reflecting on them:

- What does the statement that play should be 'an omnipresent activity in the preschool' (p. 6) mean to you?
- Should play be 'an omnipresent activity in the preschool'? (p. 6). Why? Why not?
- Reflect on the idea that democracy, respect, rights, justice, equality, and gender equality are integral parts of the play curriculum.
- What might it mean for teachers to have *goals to strive for*, rather than *goals to be attained*?
- Discuss why there is no formal assessment of individual child outcomes in terms of grades and evaluation.

Revisions to *Curriculum for the Pre-school Lpfö 98* are likely to be made soon. A draft document has been circulated and feedback is currently being gathered. Some major changes have been proposed such as including content areas with language and communication, science and technology*, and mathematics. The importance of play has been retained but mention is made of children using rules in play. Proposals also include changing the wording to *promoting* children's development and learning (rather than striving to promote it), and a move from focusing on the individual child to focusing on all involved in the preschool. The draft also introduces the notion of evaluation. It is suggested that children, teachers and parents are to be engaged in evaluating the goals and activities of the preschool and that the child's perspective is to be sought in this process. Reflective practice about the ways in which evaluation occurs is also encouraged by practitioners. The proposed changes are significant in terms of the inclusion of content areas, the move to focus

---

* Feedback to the proposed revisions to Curriculum for the Preschool Lpfö 98 was due in early 2010.

more on the group as opposed to the individual child, and the inclusion of evaluation. For now, what is included in the revised document and the areas of emphasis remains under discussion.

England

In England, the Early Years Foundation Stage (EYFS) is a play-based framework for early learning and care of children from birth to the age of five. The framework was revised in May, 2008 and replaced previous versions (e.g., *Curriculum Guidance for the Foundation Stage*; the *Birth to Three Matters* framework; *National Standards for Under 8s Daycare and Childminding*). While there are other supporting resources, the framework consists of two key documents:

- the *Statutory Framework for the Early Years Foundation Stage* (Department for Children, Schools and Families [DCSF] 2008a);
- the *Practice Guidance for the Early Years Foundation Stage* (DCSF 2008b).

Because the *Statutory Framework for the Early Years Foundation Stage* (hereafter Framework) has been enacted in legislation, all schools and early years' providers in settings registered by the Office for Standards in Education, Children's Services and Skills in England (Ofsted) attended by young children are required to use the Framework. The age range specified by the term 'young children' is from 'birth to the end of the academic year in which a child has their fifth birthday' (DCSF 2008a: 7). The Statutory Framework and Practice Guidance are aimed at 'improving outcomes and reducing inequalities' (DCSF 2008a: 7). Reducing inequalities is a strong focus of the document and is to occur through '... providing for equality of opportunity and anti-discriminatory practice and ensuring that every child is included and not disadvantaged because of ethnicity, culture or religion, home language, family background, learning difficulties or disabilities, gender or ability' (DCSF 2008a: 7).

The EYFS Statutory Framework (DCSF 2008a) is 54 pages in length and has four sections:

- introduction;
- learning and development requirements;
- welfare requirements;
- other information.

The introduction states that four principles are to guide the work of practitioners:

- a unique child;
- positive relationships;

- enabling environments;
- learning and development.

The paragraph describing learning and development indicates that these two attributes are 'equally important and inter-connected' (p. 9). A key aspect of the principled approach is the attention given to reducing inequalities. Providers must meet legislated requirements for equality of opportunity in the following way:

> Providers have a responsibility to ensure positive attitudes to diversity and difference – not only so that every child is included and not disadvantaged, but also so that they learn from the earliest age to value diversity in others and grow up making a positive contribution to society.
>
> (DCSF 2008a: 9)

In addition to positive attitudes, inclusion and valuing diversity, providers are also required to remove or help overcome barriers for children where they exist; identify early signs of need and refer appropriately; stretch and challenge all children, and irrespective of a wide range of factors of diversity, give children the 'opportunity to experience a challenging and enjoyable programme of learning and development' (DCSF 2008a: 10). While attention to the provision of equality of opportunity is commendable, there is a difference between equality of opportunity and equity. The former is about providing equal opportunities for all while equity is about fairness and justice and 'makes visible the imperative to overcome factors that potentially impede the creation of equity and equitable circumstances' (Grieshaber 2009: 92). Equity also involves power relations because it seeks a more equitable distribution of society's resources – social and economic.

   The Framework states that learning and development requirements are to be framed around play-based activities (DCSF 2008a). The early learning goals and educational programmes 'must be delivered through planned, purposeful play, with a balance of adult-led and child-initiated activities' (DCSF 2008a: 11). Reference to the balance of adult- and child-led activities reflects recent research that stresses the importance of the role of adults in children's learning (e.g., Sylva et al. 2004) as well as challenges to 'free' play that is encouraged in child-centred pedagogy, where the role of teachers is minimal. Early learning goals must be achieved by the end of the academic year in which children turn five and specified educational programmes must be taught to children (matters, skills, processes). There are requirements to assess the level of children's achievements in the six areas covered by the early learning goals and educational programmes:

- personal, social and emotional development;
- communication, language and literacy;

- problem solving, reasoning and numeracy;
- knowledge and understanding of the world;
- physical development;
- creative development.

Appendix 1 contains the Assessment Scales, which have a number of indicators under each of the six areas in which assessment is to occur.

The second document, *Practice Guidance for the Early Years Foundation Stage* (DCSF 2008b) has 116 pages and is divided into three sections:

- implementing the EYFS;
- learning and development;
- welfare requirements.

There are two appendices, the most sizeable of which is Appendix 2 – 'areas of learning and development', which consists of just over 90 pages and comprises most of the document. This detailed information is provided to assist practitioners to 'plan, observe and assess . . . activities with children based on their individual and developmental needs' (DCSF 2008b: 24). The role of practitioners is described as crucial in 'observing and reflecting on children's spontaneous play' and in extending and developing 'children's language and communication in their play' (DCSF 2008b: 7). Practitioners are advised that the Areas of Learning and Development (Appendix 2) '**should not be used as checklists**' (DCSF 2008b: 11; emphasis in original). In each of the six areas of learning and development, information is provided in tabular form about:

- children's development;
- advice for practitioners about what to look at, listen to and note;
- suggestions for effective practice;
- ideas for planning and resourcing.

The 'look, listen and note' sections of the six areas of 'learning and development' are suggestions for how formative assessment might be undertaken (DCSF 2008a: 16). There are strict procedures and requirements for assessment of children at the end of the foundation stage and a stage profile must be completed for each child at this time.

Table 7.4: Play and the *Statutory Framework for the Early Years Foundation Stage* (DCSF 2008a) and *Practice Guidance for the Early Years Foundation Stage* (DCSF 2008b) shows how play is conceptualized in these two documents in relation to the main ideas of this book. As with each of the other three countries, both documents from England identify a close connection between play, learning and development. Although enjoyment was suggested several times in the documents, there were no instances where a direct connection

Table 7.4 Play and the *Statutory Framework for the Early Years Foundation Stage* and *Practice Guidance for the Early Years Foundation Stage*

Understandings of play	*Links to the* Statutory Framework for the Early Years Foundation Stage *and* Practice Guidance for the Early Years Foundation Stage
Play as learning (see Chapter 1)	'Play underpins all development and learning for young children . . . it is through play that they develop intellectually, creatively, physically, socially and emotionally' (DCSF 2008b: 7)
Play as fun; play as hard work (see Chapter 2): '. . . play is equated with fun . . . fun is contingent on who, when and where.'	'Providing well-planned experiences based on children's spontaneous play, both indoors and outdoors, is an important way in which practitioners support young children to learn with enjoyment and challenge' (DCSF 2008b: 7)
Naturally produced play (play is children's natural way of learning) (see Chapter 3)	'Most children play spontaneously, although some may need adult support' (DCSF 2008b: 7) 'Through play, in a secure but challenging environment with effective adult support, children can: . . . practise and build up ideas, concepts and skills' (DCSF 2008b: 8) 'Play games that encourage children to link sounds to letters and words' (DCSF 2008b: 60) 'Provide materials and opportunities for children to use writing in their play' (DCSF 2008b: 60) 'plan appropriate play and learning experiences based on children's interests and needs, and identify any concerns about a child's development' (DCSF 2008b: 11)
Play as serious business (. . . turning the documentation of play into a serious business) (see Chapter 4)	'. . . you must undertake the EYFS [Early Years Foundation Stage] Profile for all children of an appropriate age and assess them through observational assessment against the 13 scales and report 13 scores for each child' (DCSF 2008b: 12)
Rules of/for play (see Chapter 5)	'Through play, in a secure but challenging environment with effective adult support, children can: . . . learn how to understand the need for rules' (DCSF 2008b: 8)
Playing fair (see Chapter 6)	'Understand what is right, what is wrong, and why' (DCSF 2008b: 36) 'Work as part of a group or class, taking turns and sharing fairly' (DCSF 2008b: 34) 'Establish opportunities for play and learning that acknowledge children's particular religious beliefs and cultural backgrounds.' (DCSF 2008b: 25)

was made between play and fun (in the same sentence). There are many suggestions in the documents that play is children's natural way of learning and for how practitioners can capitalize on this. The requirement for summative assessment of each child toward the end of the Foundation Stage is a feature of the English documents alone, as is the fact that they have been legislated, which means a legal requirement to comply by completing the stage profile for each child. Children can learn to understand the need for rules through play itself and the provision of a secure but challenging environment with adult support. Playing fair is conceptualized as taking turns and sharing, as well as being involved in play and learning that acknowledges the diversity of children's religious beliefs and cultural backgrounds.

Reflection point 7.4 focuses on some of the main ideas in the Framework and Practice Guidance documents that relate to play.

Reflection point 7.4

Discuss the following ideas with others, reflecting on them:

- What are the implications of having a document legislated by an Act of Parliament, which states that all areas of learning and development 'must be delivered through planned, purposeful play' (DCSF 2008a: 11)?
- How does equality of opportunity relate to purposeful play?
- How might practitioners enact antidiscriminatory practice and ensure that every child is included and not disadvantaged because of ethnicity, culture or religion, home language, family background, learning difficulties or disabilities, gender or ability?
- What types of assessment are possible and/or appropriate for play-based learning?

The place of play in the curriculum documents

There are some similarities and differences among the documents from the four countries and each reflects the ultimate outcome of consultation that occurred in the respective countries. The value of play permeates each document in regard to curriculum, teaching and learning approaches, pedagogical strategies and assessment (with the exception of Sweden). Specific similarities include:

- the overwhelming emphasis on play-based approaches for children aged birth to five;
- the importance of play for children's development and learning (sometimes learning and development);
- the endorsement of active roles for teachers in children's play (e.g., intentional teaching as opposed to lack of involvement or passive roles for teachers);
- the inclusion of 'content' areas in various forms, to be 'learned' through play;
- the inclusion of values to be learned through play (fairness, equality, equity);
- the importance of pedagogy associated with play;
- the emphasis on play as progress.

The conceptualization of play as learning stood out in each document, as did what we have called 'naturally produced play' (see Chapter 3). Naturally produced play is the very powerful idea that play is children's natural way of learning. The trouble with this is that play is rarely natural: it is manufactured inside and outside classrooms by teachers using curriculum documents; the aim of which is for children to learn particular content and values through play while abiding by adult-set rules. However, where play in early childhood settings might not be so closely connected to policy documents and outcomes (i.e., child-centred 'free play'), it is still manufactured in classrooms by teachers whose intention is that children develop and learn particular things through play (e.g., language, self esteem). And there are still rules.

Seeing play as progress is bound with notions of play as learning and as producing educational outcomes, which are consistently valued highly in the curriculum documents (with the exception of Sweden and the achievement of learning outcomes). All documents reviewed in this chapter made the assumption that play-based approaches would 'transfer to some other kinds of progress that are not in themselves forms of play' (Sutton-Smith 1997: 51). The same is true of 'free' play, which is considered by advocates to be different from the 'educational' type of play found in current curriculum and policy documents. We agree that there is a difference between play-based curricula that are aimed at achieving specific outcomes, and widely accepted understandings of free play (i.e., play that is freely chosen, personally driven and intrinsically motivated). Though to some it might not be quite as visible as the association between 'educational' play and progress, as Sutton-Smith (1997) notes, free play too is consumed by the rhetoric of progress as it relates to social, moral, physical and cognitive development.

In terms of social justice it doesn't matter whether it is 'educational' or 'free' play as it is still vested with relationships of power; and therefore provides opportunities for those more privileged to assert themselves in various ways, as shown in the vignettes throughout this book and in the qualitative studies that have been cited. Viewing play as progress can conceal the ways in which children construct multiple roles and identities for themselves. In Chapter 6 we shared a vignette about two children who on two different occasions used force and physically manipulated the body of a younger, smaller child of mixed heritage to take away the toys he was playing with. They did this without the teachers knowing and so preserved their identities as reputable members of the class. In a scenario from Chapter 5, the teacher told Natalie she was a 'good girl' for eating all her fruit, when in fact Natalie had deposited three pieces of fruit in the rubbish bin, being very careful to ensure that the teachers did not see her. As she was so adept at this secretive but public classroom act, we wondered whether it was a regular occurrence. In the teacher's eyes Natalie was a good girl for eating her fruit. Had Natalie been seen getting rid of the fruit, it most likely would have been a different matter. As it was, Natalie's 'good girl' identity was protected and her preference for not eating fruit was not revealed.

Seeing play as progress also makes invisible the ways in which children construct shared meanings amongst some and exclude others. In Chapter 3 we related the experience of Lulu, who, at the request of the teacher, was included by three girls playing Cinderella. Later the teacher was horrified to find that the girls had colluded and assigned Lulu the role of the 'piece of paper that was in front of the fireplace, collecting the cinders.' Children use play for their own particular means and ends, and in many cases these means and ends involve many identities, where they can position themselves more powerfully than others, sometimes so discreetly that their actions go unnoticed by staff. When teachers are focused only on the educational value of play or choose not to intervene in children's 'free play', it makes noticing or attending to unjust actions problematic. Consequently teachers can miss the intricate and complex nature of children's relationships and how they can very capably switch roles and identities to suit the situation.

The documents reviewed in this chapter all make statements about issues connected with social justice, which is commendable. To uphold these ideals is the next challenge and to do so, teachers need to know and understand:

- that play can be unfair and inequitable;
- what fair play is, how to play fair;
- how to identify unfair play and what to do about it;
- how to teach children about playing fair.

8 End play

There is much written about play, and not just in the field of education. This book makes no claims to be a comprehensive coverage of the growing body of research, literature, opinions, blogs and journalism discussing the topic with gusto. However, in the field of early childhood education, we fear we are losing the battle over play, and in some places the academic push-down has at least one foot in the door. We know that many of our colleagues share this concern. There are a number of options available to those who have a strong commitment to respecting the rights and attending to the needs of young children, and we try all of them. Strong traditions of leadership and advocacy in early childhood education have us trying new and old ways to describe, account, defend and advocate for a play-based curriculum.

Evidence suggests, however, that in some cases and places, these strategies are proving inadequate to resist the regime of standardized tests, the measurement of performance, and the publication of these measures for the purpose of comparison. In this book, we do not set up outcomes and play-based approaches as oppositional or warring factions. We reject the siege mentality. This book aims to provoke thinking, conversations, debates and disagreements. When we think and talk together, we can build more rigorous and robust understandings that can accommodate the complexities in play, and also accept that not all play is natural, fun, innocent, free. Rather, play is also about power relationships, sometimes played out obviously, sometimes more subtly. Of most concern to us in this book is to raise questions about the role of the teacher, the responsibility to attend to what is happening in play, what it is that children are learning, and understand how they are learning.

This book contains many examples of events in early childhood classrooms. They are not spectacular events, and we certainly hope we have not glamorized them or attributed false grandiosity to what was witnessed. Our point is that these events and any number of others like these are occurring every day in early childhood classrooms. It is the everyday nature and taken-for-grantedness of the events that makes them worthy of comment. When teachers invoke the mantra that 'children learn through play', this works for better and worse. The defence of play can be supported by histories, traditions and sound pedagogical principles, which can account for play as the best way for young children to learn. At the same time, we can do ourselves a disservice, when we insist that natural learning occurs as a result of play. This disallows the complexity and intensity of teachers' everyday work in early childhood settings. Anyway, if children play naturally and naturally learn through play, anyone should be able to watch over them. No qualifications required!

This final chapter is playful, and we invite you to play along with us. There is no end to the complexities of play but in this, the End Play, we bring together the key ideas raised in this book, and hope that you will continue to consider and reflect on some of the ideas we play with. There are no rules for reading this chapter, and it can be fun. What follows are a series of provocations about play, sometimes in the form of questions, sometimes with some thinking, and sometimes simply leaving the space for you to play.

1   What if play is not natural?

In Chapter 1 we introduced some of the resilient historical influences on the field of early childhood education, including Rousseau's imaginary child Émile. In Chapter 3 we discussed the discourse of the natural, and how this works to shape thinking and practices in early childhood education. What if Rousseau lived in another time and place and, instead of Émile, he imagined another child who grew up in a high rise building in the centre of a bustling metropolis? The child preferred to spend most of his time playing on a computer, and he used an avatar called Hulk to have virtual adventures. Or what if Rousseau's Émile was Émily, and she loved to run with the wolves and cut down trees? Or what if Émily had been taken forcibly from her parents when she was very young, and grew up in an institution, and was made to work from the age of three years?

How do ideas about natural childhoods shape the environment and experiences provided for children in early childhood settings, and what would change if being natural was considered a disadvantage? How might these ideas apply to some children in early childhood settings today?

2   What if play is not fun?

In Chapter 3, it seemed that play was not fun for Lulu when she was given a demeaning role in the Cinderella play – although it must be said that this is only a presumption, since we have no evidence that Lulu was upset. But it would be safe to also presume that play is not fun for the child who is bullied, rejected, excluded, or physically harmed or otherwise made to feel unsafe. On the other hand, for the bully, although this is not a palatable thought, it would seem that causing harm to others appears to be fun.

For some of us, there are forms of fun that are more fun than others. For instance, some people can imagine nothing better than spending a whole day (or even four days!) watching a single game of cricket unfold, and for others, the joys of cricket are a mystery. Cultural, social, community and family backgrounds can all be determining factors in fun. The consequences for a child who does not understand the 'rules for fun' in an early childhood setting can be substantial. What of the child who considers it fun to sweep the kitchen floor, or play chess with Uncle Ted, or spend time alone, daydreaming?

One final provocation about fun. What if children learn to perform fun, because when they appear to be having fun, they are rewarded (with attention, praise, encouragement, glamorous documentation, or perhaps the teacher leaves them alone, and this is reward enough)? Can you imagine children learning to 'do fun', because that seems to make the teacher happy, and a happy teacher is more fun than an unhappy one?

3   What if some of the environmental regulatory practices were reversed?

In Chapter 3, we discussed how it is the work of the teacher, not nature, that controls the conditions for success. What if children spent most of their time in the playground, or at 'outside' play? What would they learn? How? What would be the role of the teacher? What are the implications of this suggestion? Which children would have their chances for success improved with this change? Which children would be disadvantaged?

Climatic conditions might make this shift unsuitable for many children. But are there children for whom this would be a more appropriate way to organize the programme? In many countries in the Northern Hemisphere, it would seem that the climate dictates that children spend most of their time inside. Yet, in some Nordic early childhood settings, the children play outside, no matter the weather conditions. Do cultural factors override climate conditions? What of children in some parts of Australia, for instance, who are confined to hot, sweltering classrooms, when the cool of the breezes and the shade make outside more comfortable?

Can you imagine other regulatory practices that might be reversed, and how this would change children's behaviours and teachers' pedagogy?

4   What if standardized testing for play was introduced?

In Chapter 4, we suggested some dilemmas with assessment, and this is not a word that is prominent in the early childhood education lexicon, although medical and paediatric assessments are not troublesome. What if each child (aged 3) was tested for play skills and scores for early childhood settings were benchmarked, and published in the national newspaper? Would this work to raise the status of play? Would you do more explicit teaching, in order to support the children in meeting the play outcomes? What if your salary, or funding for the centre, was tied to your children's scores on the play test? How and what would you teach if you were accountable for delivering a play-based programme, and the children were required to pass the standardized test before they moved on to the next level?

Can play be assessed? If so, what exactly would be assessed, and how? Can you think of any reason why play would be assessed, and can you think of how this might affect your practice, in a positive way? (A reminder: we promised to ask questions that provoke discussion and debate. We did not promise to provide answers!)

5   What if children really did set the rules?

In Chapter 5, we discussed play rules, and the implicit and explicit rules in early childhood settings. It is a common practice in many early childhood settings for the teacher to invite the children's collaboration and input in the defining of 'classroom rules'. This has long been a strategy favoured by those who consider it to be part of their work to model and teach democratic principles and ideas about freedom and responsibilities. Teachers call on the discourses of values, and beliefs about relationships, trust, respect, and the competent child, to make decisions around this approach to rules.

But we have rarely seen this enacted in any genuine way in the settings we have been associated with. In most cases, the teacher facilitates a group discussion, and helps the group come to consensus on the rules for the group. The rules are usually fairly predictable, similar, and work to serve the teacher's agenda. For example, such rules might include: one person talks at a time; listen carefully; treat everyone in our room with respect; keep the room tidy. The benefits of establishing such common understandings are, of course, obvious. The trouble is, we wonder to what extent the children actually have genuine input into the composition of these rules, or whether perhaps they are the played, not the players.

Imagine if young children really did compose the rules for their setting. Of course children do have their own rules, and their own ways of claiming power and control, within their own culture (of the children). But we wonder what rules they would have for their classroom, if they genuinely did have the say in the rules. And we wonder what other regulatory practices the teacher might need to use, if the children's rules ruled. Indeed we wonder whether the teacher would abide by the rules and what would happen in the event of the rules being broken – would there be different rules if the teacher as opposed to the children 'broke' the rules?

6   What are the costs of free play?

In Chapter 6, one of the vignettes showed how play cost Abdul his friendship with Brian. Thankfully Abdul's teacher paid careful attention to the play in her classroom, and was alerted to a distressing moment for Abdul or, rather, Abdul drew her attention to his confusion. But in this book we have also made a number of observations of the activities of children that are invisible to teachers, for any number of reasons. For example, quiet children who are not 'naturally' gregarious, noisy, or even busy can escape the teacher's attention for long periods of time. Busy teachers can be unaware of much of what is happening in their settings, and Nelson's father, in Chapter 4, would be happy to hear that the panopticon surveillance (Foucault 1988) is not ever present!

But when play is free play, what is it free from? And what are the costs? The natural and fun discourses allow for the busy, happy children, but they also disallow too much 'structure' or 'intervention' from the teacher. As discussed in Chapter 6, play can be a site where children enact power relationships, and reproduce cultural and social bias and injustice. If teachers leave children to play out these agendas, and by default, allow unfair and unjust treatment of children, what are the social, emotional, physical, economic and cultural costs to all involved? In Chapter 3, we referred to Darwin's notion of survival of the fittest, and the unjust practices that this theory permits. If free play means leaving children to fend for themselves, in an environment where power imbalances are stacked against them, then what they learn is that this imbalance has been created and ignored in their early childhood setting. They learn about helplessness, and practices of exclusion, othering, bullying, gendering. They are free to resist or join in, and they learn survival strategies that may or may not be healthy and wholesome.

What is the expectation that children are learning through free play? And how free is free play? Are the children, for instance, free to invent, create, express themselves, communicate and build friendships? Or does free simply mean free from academic constraints? What are the likely costs if free play was absolutely free?

7   What if all teachers in early childhood education were required to have a three year qualification in play?

In Chapter 7, we looked at various curriculum documents across countries, and the similarities and differences amongst them. Play is an essential component common to each of the documents analysed, and this leads us to some playful ideas about teacher qualifications. Qualifications are recognized as an important contributing factor to quality teaching and quality outcomes for children. So we wondered, since play is such an important component of pedagogical practices in early childhood education, how are teachers qualified to support children's learning through play?

We have examined the many discourses that historically and currently shape pedagogy, and analysis of events in Fiona's classroom (in Chapter 3) brought us to the evidence of her work being a product of her training. We know that almost every early childhood teacher is familiar with the 'benefits of play' and can attest to play being children's natural way of learning. But, as we have shown in this book, there are complexities and contradictions within the play discourse, and what one person might call play, another might call 'gimmick', or art. If teachers were required to study for a three-year qualification in play, this could add more depth and rigor to teachers' understandings of both the benefits and the trouble with play.

A Bachelor in Play degree qualification could work to lift the status of play and early childhood education, or it could perpetuate some of the myths about the work of early childhood educators, who 'just play with the children all day'. This degree qualification could work to attract more male early childhood educators. It might be dismissed as a triviality, or have broader appeal to those in business, commerce and creative industries, who have recently turned to play and creativity as valued commodities and capacities. (Playworkers in the UK can study for a foundation degree in playwork. The theory and practice of playwork recognizes that children's play is freely chosen, personally driven, intrinsically motivated, and not subject to adult agendas.)

As we have discussed in this book, language shapes our thinking, speaking and acting, and the word 'play' acts to both value add, and detract from the importance or significance of a range of other terms. There are no 'rules' that say play is good, but consider the list of phrases below, and how the words 'play' and 'games' work to create meaning. Some of these terms may be familiar to you, and some may be so colloquial that, for you, they have little meaning. Quite simply, our point is that using the word 'play' does not capture and convey a universal concept or message. Language works powerfully to shape beliefs and practices, and it is important to understand the power of the words we use to communicate:

Playing with ideas	You're not playing
Playing with my mind	S/he plays hard
Mind games	It's just a game
Playing games	It's hard to play
Game player	Playboy
S/he's a real player	Play ball
S/he's a player	Play house
S/he's not a player	Playing it down
I'm just playing	Playing up
I'm not playing	Playing around

Playing it straight	Instant play
Best play	Fast play
Worst play	Slow play
Good play	Play fighting
Bad play	Play therapy
In play	Playground
Out of play	Playwork
Replay	Play range

We finish this chapter and this book with a final provocation for you to play with, consider, imagine, discuss, disagree, debate, and reflect on:

8   What if education was reorganized and, instead of the children coming to the teacher, teachers went to where the children were, and worked with them in their environment?

References

Ailwood, J. (2003) Governing early childhood education through play, *Contemporary Issues in Early Childhood*, 4(3): 286–99.

Bakhtin, M. (1981) Discourse in the novel, in M. Holquist (ed.) (trans. C. Emerson and M. Holquist), *The Dialogic Imagination: Four Essays by M.M. Bakhtin* (pp. 259–422). Austin: University of Texas Press.

Belfield, C.R., Nores, M., Barnett, S. and Schweinhart, L. (2006) The High/Scope Perry Preschool Program: cost-benefit analysis using data from the age-40 follow-up, *Journal of Human Resources*, 41(1): 162–90.

Bennett, N., Wood, E. and Rogers, S. (1997) *Teaching Through Play: Reception Teachers' Theories and Practice*. Buckingham: Open University Press.

Berger, J. (1982) *Ways of Seeing*. London: BBC and Penguin Books.

Blaise, M. (2005) A feminist poststructuralist study of children doing gender, *Early Childhood Research Quarterly*, 20: 85–108.

Boyd, B.J. (2002) Teacher response to superhero play, in K.M. Paciorek (ed.), *Taking Sides: Clashing Views on Controversial Issues in Early Childhood Education* (pp. 96–103). Guilford, CT: McGraw-Hill/Dushkin.

Bredekamp, S. (ed.) (1987) *Developmentally Appropriate Practice in Early Childhood Programs Serving Children from Birth Through Age 8* (expanded edn). Washington, DC: National Association for the Education of Young Children.

Bredekamp, S. and Copple, C. (eds) (1997) *Developmentally Appropriate Practice in Early Childhood Programs* (revised edition). Washington, DC: National Association for the Education of Young Children.

Bresler, L. (1993) Three orientations to arts in the primary grades: implications for curriculum reform, *Arts Education Policy Review*, 94(6): 29–34.

Brooker, L. (2002) *Starting School: Young Children Learning Cultures*. Buckingham: Open University Press.

Burman, E. (2008) *Deconstructing Developmental Psychology* (2nd edn). London: Routledge.

Burr, R. (2002) Global and local approaches to children's rights in Vietnam, *Childhood*, 9(1): 49–61.

Butler, J. (2005) Bodies that matter, in M. Fraser and M. Greco (eds), *The Body: A Reader* (pp. 62–72). London: Routledge.

Campbell, S. (2005) Secret children's business: resisting and redefining access to learning in the early childhood classroom, in N. Yelland (ed.), *Critical Issues in Early Childhood Education* (pp. 146–62). Buckingham: Open University Press.

Cannella, G.S. (1997) *Deconstructing Early Childhood Education: Social Justice and Revolution*. New York: Peter Lang.

Chan, L.K.S. and Chan, L. (2003) Early childhood education in Hong Kong and its challenges, *Early Childhood Development and Care*, 173(1): 7–17.

Cheng, D.P.W. (2001) Difficulties of Hong Kong teachers' understanding and implementation of 'play' in the curriculum, *Teaching and Teacher Education*, 17: 857–69.

Claxton, G. (2002) *Building Learning Power: Helping Young People Become Better Learners*. Bristol: TLO Limited.

Cleverley, J. and Phillips, C. (1987) *Visions of Childhood*. Sydney: Allen & Unwin.

Colker, L.J. (2008) Twelve characteristics of effective early childhood teachers, *Young Children*, 63(2): 68–73.

Commonwealth of Australia (2009) *Belonging, Being and Becoming: The Early Years Learning Framework for Australia*. Canberra: Department of Education, Employment and Workplace Relations for the Council of Australian Governments.

Cook, D. (2004) *The Commodification of Childhood: The Children's Clothing Industry and the Rise of the Child Consumer*. Durham: Duke University Press.

Copple, C. and Bredekamp, S. (eds) (2009) *Developmentally Appropriate Practice in Early Childhood Programs: Serving Children from Birth Through Age Eight* (3rd edn). Washington, DC: National Association for the Education of Young Children.

Corsaro, W.A. (1985) *Friendship and Peer Culture in the Early Years*. Norwood, NJ: Ablex Publishing.

Corsaro, W.A. and Schwartz, K. (1999) Peer play and socialisation in two cultures: implications for research and practices, in B. Scales, M. Almy, A. Nicolopoulou and S. Ervin-Tripp (eds) *Play and the Social Context of Development in Early Care and Education* (pp. 234–54). New York: Teachers College Press.

Crain, W. (2005) *Theories of Development: Concepts and Applications* (5th edn). Upper Saddle River, NJ: Pearson.

Curran, J.M. (1999) Constraints of pretend play: explicit and implicit rules, *Journal of Research in Childhood Education*, 14(1): 47–55.

Curriculum Development Council (1996) *Guide to the Pre-primary Curriculum*. Hong Kong: Government Printer.

Curriculum Development Council (2006) *Guide to the Pre-primary Curriculum*. Hong Kong: Government Printer.

Danby, S. and Baker, C. (1998) How to be masculine in the block area, *Childhood*, 5(12): 151–75.

Davies, B. (1993) *Shards of Glass: Children Reading and Writing Beyond Gendered Identities*. Sydney: Allen & Unwin.

Department for Children Schools and Families (DCSF). (2008a) *Statutory Framework for the Early Years Foundation Stage*, Nottingham: DCSF Publications.

Department for Children Schools and Families (DCSF). (2008b) *Practice Guidance for the Early Years Foundation Stage*. Nottingham: DCSF Publications.

Edwards, C., Gandini, S. and Forman, G. (1998) *The Hundred Languages of Children: The Reggio Emilia Approach to Early Childhood Education* (2nd edn). Norwood, NJ: Ablex.

Emilson, A. (2007) Young children's influence in preschool, *International Journal of Early Childhood*, 39(1): 11–38.

Fein, G.G. (1999) Reflections on rhetoric and rhetorics, in S. Reifel (ed.), *Advances in Education and Day Care: Foundations, Adult Dynamics, Teacher Education and Play Vol. 10* (pp. 189–99). Stamford, CT: JAI Press.

Florida, R. (2003) *The Rise of the Creative Class*. Sydney: Pluto Press.

Foucault, M. (1988) Technologies of the Self, in H. Gutman, L.H. Martin and P.H. Hutton (eds), *Technologies of the Self: A Seminar with Michel Foucault*. Amherst, MA: University of Massachusetts Press.

Foucault, M. (2000) Governmentality, in J.D. Faubion (ed.), *Power: The Essential Works of Foucault 1954–1984* (pp. 201–22). London: Penguin.

Froebel, F. (1900) *The Education of Man* (revised edition) (trans. D. Appleton). Clifton NJ: Augustus M. Kelly Publishers.

Fung, C.K.H. and Lee, J.C.K. (2008) A critical review of the early childhood education (ECE) curriculum documents in Hong Kong, *Journal of Basic Education*, 17(1): 33–56.

Giugni, M. (2008) Observations on the public and the private in early childhood settings. Presentation in the Research and Scholarship Series, School of Early Childhood, Queensland University of Technology, Brisbane, September.

Giugni, M (n.d.), *Exploring Multiculturalism, Anti Bias and Social Justice in Children's Services*. Sydney: Professional Support Coordination Unit and Children's Services Central.

Grieshaber, S. (2008a) Fun, play-based education, *Every Child*, 14(3): 30–1.

Grieshaber, S. (2008b) Interrupting stereotypes: teaching and the education of young children, *Early Education and Development*, 19(3): 505–18.

Grieshaber, S. (2009) Equity and quality in the early years of school, *Curriculum Perspectives*, 29(1): 91–7.

Gunnarson, L. (2007a) Early childhood education in Sweden, in R.S. New and M. Cochran (eds), *Early Childhood Education: An International Encyclopedia* (pp. 1240–6). Westport, CT: Praeger.

Gunnarson, L. (2007b) Quality in Swedish early childhood education, in R.S. New and M. Cochran (eds), *Early Childhood Education: An International Encyclopedia* (pp. 1258–61). Westport, CT: Praeger.

Hampton, M. (2002) Limiting superhero play in preschool classrooms, in K M. Paciorek (ed.), *Taking Sides: Clashing Views on Controversial Issues in Early Childhood Education* (pp. 86–95). Guilford, CT: McGraw-Hill/Dushkin.

Hendrick, H. (1997) Constructions and reconstructions of British childhood: an interpretive survey, 1800 to the present, in A. James and A. Prout (eds), *Constructing and Reconstructing Childhood: Contemporary Issues in the Sociological Study of Childhood* (2nd edn) (pp. 34–62). London: Falmer.

Holland, P. (2003) *We Don't Play with Guns Here: War, Weapon and Superhero Play in the Early Years*. Maidenhead: Open University Press.

Honig, A.S. (2007) Play: ten power boosts for children's early learning, *Young Children*, 62(5): 72–8.

Hubbard, R. (1994) *Authors of Pictures, Draughtsmen of Words*. New York: Heinemann.

Hyland, N. (in press). Intersections of race and sexuality in a teacher education course, *Teaching Education*.

James, A., Jenks, C. and Prout, A. (1998) *Theorizing Childhood*. New York: Teachers College Press.

Johnson, R. (2000) *Hands off! The Disappearance of Touch in the Care of Children*. New York: Peter Lang.

Kane, P. (2004) *The Play Ethic: A Manifesto for a Different Way of Living*. London: Macmillan.

King, N. (1992) The impact of context on the play of young children, in S. Kessler and B. Swadener (eds), *Reconceptualizing the Early Childhood Curriculum: Beginning the Dialogue* (pp. 43–61). New York: Teachers College Press.

Knight, L. (2008) Communication and transformation through collaboration: rethinking drawing activities in early childhood, *Contemporary Issues in Early Childhood*, 9(4): 306–16.

Lau, W.C.M. (2006) Strategies kindergarten teachers use to enhance children's musical creativity: case studies of three Hong Kong teachers. Unpublished PhD thesis. Queensland University of Technology, Brisbane, Australia.

Lee, J.S. (2006) Preschool teachers shared beliefs about appropriate pedagogy for 4-year-olds, *Early Childhood Education Journal*, 33(6): 433–41.

Li, Y.L. (2003) What makes a good kindergarten teacher? A pilot interview study in Hong Kong, *Early Child Development and Care*, 173(1): 19–31.

Li, Y.L. (2004) The culture of teaching in the midst of Western influence: the case of Hong Kong kindergartens, *Contemporary Issues in Early Childhood*, 5(3): 330–48.

Luke, A. and Grieshaber, S. (2004) New adventures in the politics of literacy: an introduction, *Journal of Early Childhood Literacy*, 4(1): 5–9.

McArdle, F.A. (2003) The visual arts, in S. Wright (ed.), *The Arts, Young Children and Learning* (pp. 151–81). Boston: Pearson Education.

McArdle, F. (2008) The arts and staying cool, *Contemporary Issues in Early Childhood*, 9(4): 365–74.

McArdle, F. and Tan, J. (2009) Arts project with refugee children: art as pedagogy and method. Paper presented at the European Early Childhood Education Research Association conference, Strasbourg, France, August.

McArdle, F. and Wong, B. (2009) *Asking young children about art: A comparative study*. Paper presented at 3rd International Art(s) in Early Childhood Conference, Singapore, June 1–3, 2009.

MacNaughton, G. and Davis, K. (2001) Beyond 'othering': rethinking approaches to teaching young Anglo-Australian children about indigenous Australians, *Contemporary Issues in early Childhood*, 2(1): 83–93.

McWilliam, E. and Jones, A. (2005) An unprotected species? Teachers as risky subjects, *British Educational Research Journal*, 31(1): 109–20.

Miles, L.R. (2009) The general store: reflections on children at play, *Young Children*, 64(4): 36–41.

Montessori, M. (1965) *Dr Montessori's Own Handbook*. New York: Schocken Books.

Mundine, K. and Giugni, M. (2006) *Diversity and Difference: Lighting the Spirit of Identity*. Watson, ACT: Early Childhood Australia.

Nieto, S. and Bode, P. (2008) *Affirming Diversity: The Sociopolitical Context of Multicultural Education* (5th edn). Boston, MA: Pearson.

Opper, S. (1992) *Hong Kong's Young Children: Their Preschools and Families*. Hong Kong: Hong Kong University Press.

Organisation for Economic Co-operation and Development (OECD) (2006) *Starting Strong II: Early Childhood Education and Care*. Paris: OECD.

Pink, D. (2005) *A Whole New Mind*. New York: Penguin.

Postman, N. (1994) *The Disappearance of Childhood*. New York: Vintage Books.

Pramling Samuelsson, I. and Johansson, E. (2009) Why do children involve teachers in their play and learning? *European Early Childhood Education Research Journal*, 17(1): 77–94.

Reineke, J., Sonsteng, K. and Gartrell, D. (2008) Nurturing mastery motivation: no need for rewards, *Young Children*, 63(6): 89–97.

Rousseau, J.J. (1762/2007) *Emile, or On Education* (trans. B Foxley) Auckland NZ: The Floating Press, www.qut.eblib.com.au.ezp01.library.qut.edu.au/EBLWeb/patron/ (accessed 11 September 2009).

Rudd, K. (2008) *Education Revolution*, http://www.pm.gov.au/topics/education.cfm (accessed 9 April 2008).

Rutter, J. (2005) *Refugee Children in the UK*. Maidenhead: Open University Press.

Ryan, S.K. (2005) Freedom to choose: examining children's experiences in choice time, in N. Yelland (ed.), *Critical Issues in Early Childhood Education* (pp. 99–114). Maidenhead: Open University Press.

Ryan, S.K. and Grieshaber, S. (2005) Shifting from developmental to postmodern practices in early childhood teacher education, *Journal of Teacher Education*, 56(1): 34–45.

Sandseter, E.H.S. (2009) Children's expressions of exhilaration and fear in risky play, *Contemporary Issues in Early Childhood*, 10(2): 92–106.

Shiller, V.M. and O'Flynn, J.C. (2008) Using rewards in the early childhood classroom: a reexamination of the issues, *Young Children*, 63(6): 88–93.

Silin, J.G. (1995) *Sex Death and the Education of Children: Our Passion for Ignorance in the Age of Aids*. New York: Teachers College Press.

Siraj-Blatchford, I. (1994) *The Early Years: Laying the Foundations for Racial Equity*. Staffordshire: Trentham Books.

Siraj-Blatchford, I. and Sylva, K. (2004) Researching pedagogy in English pre-schools, *British Educational Research Journal*, 30(5): 712–30.

Skattebol, J. (2005) Insider/outsider belongings: traversing the borders of whiteness in early childhood, *Contemporary Issues in Early Childhood*, 6(2): 189–203.

Stephens, S. (1995) *Children and the Politics of Culture*. Princeton: Princeton University Press.

Sumsion, J. (2000) Oppositional discourses: deconstructing responses to investigations of male early childhood educators, *Contemporary Issues in Early Childhood*, 1(3): 259–75.

Sutton-Smith, B. (1997) *The Ambiguity of Play*. Cambridge, MA: Harvard University Press.

Swedish Ministry of Education and Science (1994) *Curriculum for the Compulsory School System, The Pre-school Class and the Leisure-time Center – Lpo 94*. Stockholm: Swedish Ministry of Education and Science.

Swedish Ministry of Education and Science (2006) *Curriculum for the Pre-school Lpfö 98*. Stockholm: Swedish Ministry of Education and Science.

Sylva, K., Melhuish, E., Sammons, P., Siraj-Blatchford, I. and Taggart, B. (2004) *The Effective Provision of Pre-school Education: The Final Report*. London: DfES Sure Start Publications & The Institute of Education.

Thorne, B. (1993) *Gender Play: Boys and Girls in School*. Buckingham: Open University Press.

Thorpe, K., Tayler, C., Bridgstock, R., Grieshaber, S., Skoien, P., Danby, S. and Petriwskyi, A. (2004) *Preparing for School: Report of the Queensland Preparing for School Trials 2003/4*. Brisbane: Department of Education and the Arts.

Tyler, D. (1993) Making better children, in D. Meredyth and D. Tyler (eds), *Child and Citizen: Genealogies of Schooling and Subjectivity* (pp. 35–60). Brisbane: Institute for Cultural Policy Studies, Griffith University.

United Nations (1989) *Convention on the Rights of the Child*. New York: United Nations.

Vandenbroeck, M. (2009) Diversity, inclusion, and the values of democracy: building teachers' competences for intercultural education. Keynote address, European Early Childhood Education Research Association, nineteenth annual conference, Strasbourg, France, August.

Vickerius, M. and Sandberg, A. (2006) The significance of play and the environment around play, *Early Child Development and Care*, 176(2): 207–17.

Wagner, J.T. (2006) An outsider's perspective: childhoods and early childhood education in the Nordic countries, in J. Einarsdottir and J.T. Wagner (eds), *Nordic Childhoods and Early Education: Philosophy, Research, Policy and Practice in Denmark, Finland, Iceland, Norway, and Sweden* (pp. 289–306). Greenwich, CT: Information Age Publishing.

Walker, K. (2006) Playtime is the right time, *EQ Australia*, 3: 50–1.

Walkerdine, V. (1981) Sex power and pedagogy, *Screen Education*, 38: 14–21.

Walkerdine, V. (1984) Developmental psychology and the child-centred pedagogy:

the insertion of Piaget into early education, in J. Henriques, W. Hollway, C. Urwin, C. Venn and V. Walkerdine (eds), *Changing the Subject: Psychology, Social Regulation and Subjectivity* (pp. 153–202). London: Methuen.

Weber, E. (1984) *Ideas Influencing Early Childhood Education: A Theoretical Analysis.* New York: Teachers College Press.

Welsch, J.G. (2008) Playing within and beyond the story: encouraging book-related pretend play, *The Reading Teacher*, 62(2): 138–48.

Williams, P. (2001) Preschool routines, peer learning and participation, *Scandinavian Journal of Educational Research*, 45(4): 317–39.

Wong, K.S.T. (2006) A case study of leadership of kindergarten principals in Hong Kong. Unpublished PhD thesis, Queensland University of Technology, Brisbane, Australia.

Wood, E. (2007a) New directions in play: consensus or collision? *Education 3–13*, 35(4): 309–20.

Wood, E. (2007b) Reconceptualising child-centred education: contemporary directions in policy, theory and practice in early childhood, *Forum*, 49(1–2): 119–33.

Wood, E. (2009) Conceptualising a pedagogy of play: international perspectives from theory, policy and practice, in D. Kuschner (ed.), *From Children to Red Hatters®: Diverse Images and Issues of Play. Play and Culture Studies, Vol. 8* (pp. 166–89). Lanham: University Press of America, Lanham.

Wood, E. and Attfield, J. (2005) *Play, Learning and the Early Childhood Curriculum* (2nd edn). London: Paul Chapman Publishing.

Wright, S. (2003) *The Arts, Young Children, and Learning*. Boston: Allyn & Bacon.

Wright, S. (2007) Young children's meaning-making through drawing and 'telling': analogies to filmic textual features, *Australian Journal Early Childhood*, 32(4): 5–11.

Name index

Subject index

Related books from Open University Press

Purchase from www.openup.co.uk or order through your local bookseller

ENGAGING PLAY

Liz Brooker and Suzy Edwards
(Editors)

978-0-335-23586-5 (Paperback)
2010

eBook also available

This insightful edited collection brings together the perspectives of leading and emerging scholars in early childhood education and play from within Europe, the UK, Australia, New Zealand and the USA.

The chapters cover a wide range of contexts, from child-led activity in informal settings to the more formal practice of school-based learning. A range of theoretical viewpoints of play are considered and related to the experiences of today's families, children and educators across different educational settings.

Engaging Play offers an insight into the pedagogical play discourse of twenty-first century early childhood education, and in doing so offers an informative reading experience for students, researchers and policy makers alike.

www.openup.co.uk

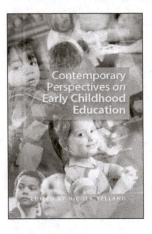

CONTEMPORARY PERSPECTIVES ON EARLY CHILDHOOD EDUCATION

Nicola Yelland (Editor)

978-0-335-23787-6 (Paperback)
2010

eBook also available

This book considers and interrogates a range of new and critical issues in contemporary early childhood education. It discusses both fundamental and emerging topics in the field, and presents them in the context of reflective and contemporary frameworks.

Bringing together leading experts whose work is at the cutting edge of contemporary early childhood education theory and research across the world, this book considers the care and education of young children from a global perspective and deals with issues and groups of children or families that are often marginalized.

This edited collection is essential reading for anyone studying or working in early childhood education.

www.openup.co.uk

OPEN UNIVERSITY PRESS
McGraw - Hill Education

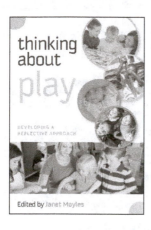

THINKING ABOUT PLAY

Janet Moyles (Editor)

978-0-335-24108-8 (Paperback)
2010

eBook also available

This edited collection brings together play and reflective practice and supports practitioners in reflecting more deeply on the play provision they make for young children. This involves analysing and evaluating what makes quality play and learning experiences by considering how current research might impact on practice.

Key features:

- Introduces the concept of 'playful pedagogies' and explains how it relates to practice
- Each chapter starts with an abstract so that readers can dip into issues of particular interest and concern
- Includes questions and follow-up ideas that can be used for CPD experiences and training

This important book supports early years students and practitioners in developing their own thinking, ideologies and pedagogies.

www.openup.co.uk

OPEN UNIVERSITY PRESS
McGraw · Hill Education